GARDENS OF THE ITALIAN VILLAS

GARDENS
OF THE
ITALIAN
VILLAS

MARELLA AGNELLI

IN ASSOCIATION WITH

LUCA PIETROMARCHI
ROBERT EMMETT BRIGHT
FEDERICO FORQUET

RIZZOLI
NEW YORK

CONTENTS

frontispiece
*A view of the parterre through a Renaissance doorway at Giardino
Giusti in Verona, Veneto.*

overleaf *The great stone mask that marks the entrance to the
Sacred Grove of Bomarzo. The gaping mouth is inscribed with the words
'Ogni pensiero vola' (Every thought flies).*

page 8 *A detail of the grotto at Villa Medici, Castello, Tuscany.*

page 10 *A moss-covered mask at Villa Lante della Rovere, Lazio.*

*Reproduced on the following pages are details of paintings by Andrea
Mantegna: 12 and 16–17 Parnassus (The Louvre, Paris): 14–15 Agony
in the Garden (National Gallery, London); 18–19 Enthroned Madonna
and Child (central panel of S. Zeno altarpiece, Verona); 20–21 Madonna
of the Victory (The Louvre, Paris); 22–23 Trivulzio Madonna (Sforzesco
Castle, Milan).*

First published in the United States of America in 1987 by
Rizzoli International Publications, Inc.
597 Fifth Avenue, New York, NY 10017

Text copyright © Marella Agnelli, Federico Forquet
and Luca Pietromarchi
Photographs copyright © Robert Emmett Bright and
Marella Agnelli

Library of Congress Cataloging-in-Publication Data

Agnelli, Marella.
Gardens of the Italian Villas.
Bibliography: p.
Includes index.
1. Gardens—Italy—Design—History.
2. Gardens, Italian—History.   I. Forquet,
Federico.   II. Pietromarchi, Luca.
III. Bright, Robert Emmett.   IV. Title.
V. Title: Italian villas.
SB466.18A35   1987   712'.6'0945   86–31532
ISBN 0–8478–0825–4

Printed and bound in Italy

PREFACE BY MARELLA AGNELLI

WHAT IS A GARDEN?

'Les vrais paradis sont les paradis que nous avons perdus' –
'The true paradises are those we have lost' – Proust reminds us.

The first garden was named Paradise, and it was also the first one we lost. But the gardens deep in our childhood, those of our parents or grandparents, or city parks where we were taken to play, remain with us only as memories, and they by definition become lost gardens of paradise.

The garden of my childhood had box and laurel hedges and an alley of cypress trees, but informal lawns and wild roses too; it was partly Italian and partly English in style, in the taste of the small Anglo-American colony to which my mother's family belonged, a colony that had settled at that time in the hillside villas around Florence.

'Children, go and call Gino. He's at the bottom of the kitchen garden, as usual. Tell him to come and water these poor roses.' This recurrent plea from our mother symbolized her own conception of the garden and the very different view of it held by Gino Guarnieri, the gardener. Gino was the youngest son of a large peasant family, and had come to us as an under-gardener when he was still practically a child. Having been sent away from home while his older brothers worked with their father in the fields had convinced him that the work he did for us was comparatively pointless and the garden itself of minor importance. It existed only because of my mother's passion for it, and it was far less important than the apple orchard or the fields to which he belonged. My own concept of a garden is the result of these two very different points of view. From my mother I learnt that a garden is a place of pleasures and surprises, a source of pride and of a sense of achievement, and that at certain times it can create a feeling of inner peace and quiet contemplation. From Gino I understood that a garden is something superfluous and unnecessary, demanding hard work for ephemeral results: its spectacular blooms last only for a brief moment after years of care and attention and one or two seasons of neglect can bring everything to ruin. But in this very quality of fragile, transitory beauty and unreality is the poetic essence of a garden.

The dictionary defines a garden as 'a place surrounded by a wall or hedge, where flowers, trees etc. are grown for delight and not for profit'. And it is this sense of delight that my friends and I would like to share with you through the pages of this book.

Behind each of these gardens there is a long, long story which interweaves the poetical ideals, the sense of elegance and all the imaginative spirit of the Italian civilization, and at last – who knows? – maybe recreates the Paradise lost . . .

A special thank you to George Weidenfeld for having given to my friends and me the opportunity to carry out this lovely project, and once more my grateful thanks to all the owners of the villas who offered us such a warm welcome and such generous hospitality.

Turin, 1987

INTRODUCTION
BY
LUCA PIETROMARCHI

COURTLINESS AND MEDITATION

The most evocative representation of the spirit of the medieval garden is to be found in the San Zenone chapel in the church of Santa Prassede in Rome. The elegant interweaving of circular patterns on the floor – 'the emerald fields of Thessalian marble, the anemones, lilies and roses of Phrygian marble' (Gnoli) – blend into a shining and resplendent image of the Garden of Paradise, as the chapel came to be known. These intricate designs also represent the natural world that flourished in the Garden of Eden; the voice of the Lord was heard as he walked 'in the garden in the cool of the day' (Genesis III:8) and the gates, according to Christian belief, were reopened to man after Christ's sacrifice. As a breviary dating from the first half of the fourteenth century declares, 'The Garden of Eden was so withered that He bathed it with His most precious blood which was shed for that garden.' The hope held out to mankind was embodied in the image of a garden re-flowering. This is the spiritual essence that permeates the silence of medieval monastic gardens, and which issues from the garden in *The Annunciation* by Fra Angelico. They are places of prayer and meditation where nature represents the recovered purity and innocence reflected in the Litanies of our Lady: *'Plantatio rosae, lilius inter spinas, fons hortorum, hortus conclusus'* (Rose garden, lily between thorns, fountain of gardens, garden enclosed).

The design of medieval gardens was to find its model in the treatise by Pietro de' Crescenzi (1230–1305), *Liber ruralium commodorum*, which marks the rebirth of the art of gardening in the late Middle Ages. (It discusses three types of garden: the small herb or flower garden, the medium-sized garden, and gardens of more than twenty acres belonging to monarchs and the very rich.) Both in the ducal and princely courts and in palaces of the period, gardens

served principally domestic purposes and comprised an orchard, a herb garden and a vegetable garden. Gradually, however, they were enriched and refined into places of pleasure and amusement, the scenes of tournaments and chivalrous amours such as were celebrated in the songs of Folgore da San Gimignano: 'Damsels dance, knights joust ... through squares, through gardens and orchards.' Crescenzi writes that orchards, protected by high walls, were planted with 'every kind of aromatic herb, rue, sage, basil, and flowers from all regions like violets, lilies, stocks'. Crusaders brought home new essences, and flowers such as iris and jasmine, as well as new ideas for garden design which were derived from the influence of the Moorish gardens they had seen on their travels. The spiritual flavour of the cloister gave way to the hedonism of the court garden; prayer books were replaced by chivalric romances; the *fons salutatis*, or fountain of salvation, of the monastic gardens became Boccaccio's 'clear fountain whose beauty brings delight and joyfulness', and whose 'basin of whitest marble, exquisitely engraved', stands in the garden where the company gathers at the beginning of the Third Day of the *Decameron*. This garden was described as 'of wondrous beauty ... walled all round ... with the richest greenery, orange trees and cedars', and the sides 'were enclosed by roses white and red, and jasmine'. It was a sanctuary from the outside world, a secret universe which harboured an image of nature as a place of gentle sensuality devoid of mysteries.

The garden became a metaphor for a natural world which man could organize and display according to his will, and for the pleasure of his senses and his spirit. 'I have seen gardens', wrote Petrarch, 'that pleased me deeply. One kind is shady, made for contemplation and consecrated to Apollo. The other is less austere and is dedicated to Bacchus.' These are the two gods that dwell in the shadows of fifteenth-century gardens. Sadly, few traces of these cloistered courtyards remain today, but evocative representations are to be found in literary descriptions and paintings of the period and it must be left to them to convey their atmosphere and spirit.

REFLECTIONS OF AN IDEAL WORLD

It was in the fifteenth century that the conflict between town life, based on commerce and power struggles, and the natural desire for peace and quiet identified with life in the country began to acquire a more profound significance. The concept of commerce and trade was set against the humanistic idea of study and contemplation, just as the unhealthiness of the city environment was contrasted with the purity of fresh country air. From these conflicts arose the notion of 'villa life', based originally on a longing for a healthy environment in which culture could flourish. 'In villa life', wrote Leon Battista Alberti (1404–72), architect and universal man of the Renaissance, 'you will enjoy pure and airy days, open and happy.'

The fifteenth-century garden was a place cut off from everyday life, an undefiled space which fulfilled a dream of an ideal world where nature was ordered and harmonious.

The sweet sensuality of medieval court gardens continued to flourish, but nature was invested with a cultural value: to stroll beneath trellised vines, among rose gardens and laurel hedges, was to penetrate a close-knit tissue of mythological allusions which the contemporary rediscovery of classical writers helps to decipher. The gardens described by Lorenzo de' Medici and praised by the poet and humanist Angelo Poliziano (1454–94) in his masterpiece *Stanze per la giostra del Magnifico Giuliano de' Medici* (Stanzas for the tournament of the Magnificent Giuliano de' Medici), which refers to

'holy and sacred flowers' – such as later appeared in the background of Botticelli's *Primavera* – were inspired by the poetry of Ovid, by the Elysian Fields described by Virgil in the Sixth Book of the Aeneid, the 'glad and quiet place' which Homer had already portrayed: this was paradise, a place of everlasting spring ruffled by the whispering of a gentle wind.

It is this classical image of nature which was reflected in the humanistic garden, filled with marble statues and historical references, and combining Chinese tradition and Greek mythology. In these surroundings the intellectual coteries of the day would gather, first and foremost the Accademia Platonica, whose members included Marsilio Ficino, Poliziano, Alberti and Pico della Mirandola, who met in the Villa Medici gardens of Careggi and the Oricellari Gardens in Florence. 'In the academic gardens, the poet listens under the laurels to the song of Apollo', wrote Ficino. Nature was seen as a mirror in which the order of a perfect and divine reality was reflected. It was that order which the art of gardening was to discover and extol. This was the source of the formal geometric tradition in the Italian garden, which was developed in the late fifteenth century in the wake of humanistic studies of harmonious proportions. As the Sienese artist and architect Francesco di Giorgio Martini (1439–1502) wrote at the end of the century, gardens must be composed of 'perfect figures, such as circles, squares or triangles,

ART, ARTIFICE AND NATURE

pentagons, hexagons or right angles'. This mathematical dream finds its highest expression in the tale attributed to Francesco Colonna in the strange romance known as *Hypnerotomachia Poliphili* (1499; *The Dream of Poliphilus*). There the Isle of Venus is a garden comprised of twenty concentric circles with marble gates and red and white marble posts covered with climbing ivy, illustrating the concept of a natural world adapted to architectural principles. As Alberti proposed, 'circles, semicircles and other geometrical figures found in the field of building will be used ... rows of trees are to be set out in lines, with equal spacing between them and with corresponding angles.'

Laid out on a central line with the façade of a villa, gardens were planned on a single linear perspective. Great attention was paid to the treatment of colonnades and open galleries, pavilions and balustrades, which linked the garden to the main body of the villa. The plants themselves were trimmed into geometrical or figurative shapes, as in the Villa Quaracchi garden in Florence designed for Giovanni Rucellai by Alberti, where the art of topiary attains a level of astonishing virtuosity, with box hedges cut in the shapes of dragons, diamonds, dolphins, cardinals and centaurs. Looking at this garden Rucellai marvelled at all its 'ordered, composed and well-proportioned features'. In them, 'his eye found a consolation which the pen cannot describe'.

The lessons of Alberti bore their most magnificent fruits in the first half of the sixteenth century, when gardening became, especially in the great Roman gardens, far more than an arrangement of trees and flowers; it developed into an art form, an expression of order, symmetry and classical austerity. 'Things that are built', wrote the sixteenth-century sculptor Baccio Bandinelli, 'must influence and predominate over things that are planted.'

Gardens took on the function of extending the architectural plan of a villa into the spaces outside, softening what would otherwise be a startling contrast between the formality of the building and the disorder of the natural world around it. The architecture of the villa transmitted its order and the rhythm of its lines to the garden, which repeated and accentuated them by means of a highly articulated arrangement of slopes, terraces and stairways. No natural or artificial element in the garden was given a particular intrinsic importance, but served to confirm and enhance the patterns and cadences of an architectural design which extended from the villa to the most distant horizons.

The finest example of this concept was Bramante's Belvedere courtyard in the Vatican (begun in 1505). In order to connect the papal palace to the villa known as the Belvedere, built by Innocent VIII on a nearby hill, Bramante squared off and terraced the slope into three vast embankments linked by a series of grand stairways.

The palace and the villa were then joined by two lateral loggias, and at the end a large niche was carved out as a centrepiece where the linear perspective of the entire work was focused. The spatial balance of the original conception was upset by the construction of a wing of the Vatican Library by Sixtus V in 1580, but the garden nonetheless served as a prototype. Its design was adopted by princes and cardinals for their villas in and around Rome – by Agostino Chigi for the Farnesina, by Giulio de' Medici for Villa Madama, for Villa d'Este in Tivoli; it provided a model for Villa Mattei in Rome, Palazzo Farnese in Caprarola, Villa Lante in Bagnaia and Villa Imperiale in Pesaro. In these great gardens architecture extends into the landscape without interruption, resolving into majestic, well composed stage sets glorifying the power, magnificence and wealth of the owner of the property.

Statues of mythological gods and goddesses were set out according to allegorical schemes, whose subject was always the glory of the prince, duke or cardinal who reigned over the estate, emphasizing not only the aesthetic and scenic but also the ideological aspects of the garden. Belvederes were placed on elevations from which the owner could enjoy a sweeping panorama of nature at his command. A raised viewpoint also made it possible, through a simple optical illusion, to create the impression of a boundless property whose centre was the villa and its garden.

In the second half of the century the secure belief in man's absolute power over nature began to falter. In the literature and painting of the time the image of an orderly, disciplined natural world seems to have gradually crumpled under the impact of some uncontrollable force. Nature came to be represented as a secret and magical universe which could excite fear and surprise, a world that both charmed and frightened. These conflicting emotions influenced the character of the gardens of the time, which exemplified aspects of the development of Mannerism, in which the strict rules of proportion and harmony that characterized Renaissance art and architecture were wilfully distorted and a new emphasis was placed on emotional expressiveness. They were places of fantastic visions, strewn, as Pirro Ligorio (1500–83), who was consulted on the design of the Villa d'Este gardens, remarks, 'with fanciful forms which, as in dreams, were conceived to inspire awe and wonder'.

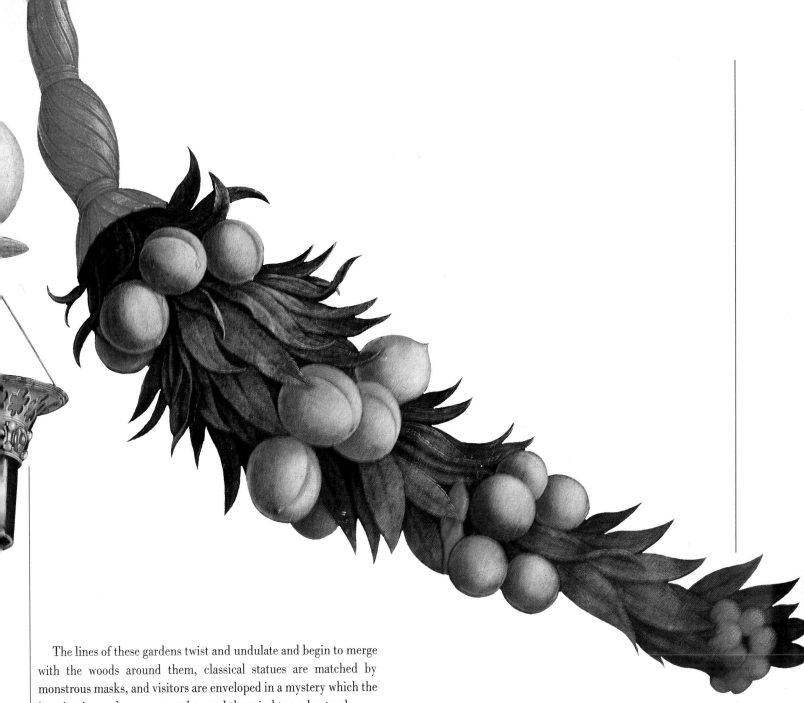

The lines of these gardens twist and undulate and begin to merge with the woods around them, classical statues are matched by monstrous masks, and visitors are enveloped in a mystery which the imagination seeks to contemplate and the mind to understand.

Gardening had always aimed to organize nature in accordance with an architectural order, but now it also began to accentuate and exploit what Eugenio Battisti calls 'the magic of the elements'. To this end groves and fountains abounded, and grottoes became a common feature of the gardens of the day. Adorned with stalactites, shells and fossils which summoned up geological and maritime mysteries, they presented a vision of the nocturnal depths of the earth. The energy and violence of nature was demonstrated by the power of jets of water that spurted and gushed forth from fountains representing islands and mountains, animals and gigantic figures. '*Le acque partono, volgono, menano, rompono*' (Waters issue forth, turn, thrash and break), as Claudio Tolomei writes, and as the cascade of the Villa Aldobrandini demonstrates.

In these gardens art in no way yields to nature; while endeavouring to discipline the landscape and contain it in geometrical patterns, it also explores and reveals the mysteries of nature by imitating its marvels. To the passion for clear logical order was added a spirit of scientific experiment in which the architect became a hydraulic engineer. An example of this trend was the Florentine Mannerist Bernardo Buontalenti (1536–1608), who in the gardens of Pratolino, north-east of Florence, created for Francesco I de' Medici a laboratory of the natural sciences in which art blended with nature in perfect harmony (sadly, the gardens were altered in 1819). Gardens of this age of innovation were strewn with self-propelled automatons, with hydraulic organs that imitated the rustling of the wind and mechanical fountains that sprinkled artificial rain. These man-made elements created the paradoxical image of a contrived but spontaneous nature. 'Art was so blended with nature', wrote Tolomei in a letter of 1543, 'that one could not discern whether the fountains were the product of the former or the latter. Thus some appeared to be a naturalistic artifice while others seemed an artifice of nature.' This feeling of uncertainty and bewilderment underlies the inscription on a stone sphinx at Bomarzo: 'Then tell me if such marvels are the result of deception or of art.'

DRAMA AND DELIGHT

While gardening in the Renaissance period set out to master nature and explore its mysteries, in the course of the seventeenth century the emphasis shifted from a desire to know and understand the natural world to one in which the main motivation was an urge to show off its wonders and enchantments on a grand and theatrical scale. Nature seems to have been regarded as a source of endlessly spectacular marvels which art set out not to codify but to glorify. The famous lines from the epic poem *Gerusalemme liberata* (1581; *Jerusalem Liberated*) by Torquato Tasso (1544–95) describe the gardens of the island of the sorceress Armida:

> So with the rude the polished mingled was
> That natural seemed all and every part:
> Nature would Craft in counterfeiting pass,
> And Imitate her imitator, Art.

Gardens became opportunities for drama and effect. It is as if the garden of Armida was cast under a sudden spell and vanished into the sea, and we are left with an idea of a garden as an ephemeral marvel, a magical place offering not so much the quiet of repose as a thrill to the imagination and the senses. Great Roman baroque gardens, such as those of Villa Pamphili and Villa Borghese, were designed not to receive princely courts for long periods of relaxation but specifically as places in which to spend a day and enjoy an entertainment before returning to everyday life. So gardens had to be as dazzling as dreams and once the festivities were over could fade into obscurity, like the garden of Armida, until next required. For the garden of the Villa Pamphili in Rome Borromini conceived, without being able to carry out, a particularly grandiose project by which, 'the guests having enjoyed the garden in the morning by strolling there, it would be possible to flood the shady paths while they were dining [so that] rising from table, they could go everywhere in little boats, which would turn out most wonderful.' Most wonderful too was Count Carlo Borromeo's transformation of Isola Bella on Lake Maggiore into a garden that seems to glide on the surface of the water.

The clear orderly plan reflecting nature's rhythms, which was typical of sixteenth-century gardens, was developed in the age of baroque into a reflection of a more complex, wider universe. Formal logic was by no means forgotten or abandoned but alongside it emerged a desire for the scenic and picturesque, an urge to replace linear perspectives by open views; lines began to falter and dissolve into natural forms, and areas of light and shade lost their sharp definition. The woods, which in sixteenth-century gardens provided the framework for a contained design, took over more and more of the garden, distorted perspectives, blocked views, and brought mystery and shadows where there was once only light and clarity.

The spirit of the age perceived that energy in nature which governs the cycles and destiny of all forms of life, and the baroque garden became a theatre in which this natural force was displayed and celebrated. Stones covered with moss turned into forms resembling vegetables, oozed drops of water and became fountains in a process of constant metamorphosis. It was no accident that the baroque imagination was especially fascinated by the myth of Daphne who, pursued by Apollo, changes into a laurel tree, an allegory which invests nature with a divine but capricious spirit.

The innumerable waterworks that had ornamented gardens since the sixteenth century can similarly be seen as the artistic expression of a capricious spirit. In 1670 Daniello Bartoli described the waters of Villa d'Este as 'extending so transparently and smoothly as to resemble the sheerest veils floating in the air, and spraying into minute drops that form a dewy cloud ... They seem to gush from underground, to leap up and hover in the air, to moan like those in pain, to bellow like the enraged and sing like the merry.'

Water became a kaleidoscope of interweaving shapes, and an endless source of interest and entertainment. It was difficult to visit one of these gardens without being soaked from head to foot, such was the mischievous care employed in hiding and disguising devices which would take the visitor by surprise with a sudden quick splash or trap him in a cage of water. A virtuoso inventor of *giochi d'acqua*, or water jokes, was Vincenzo Vincenzi, the fountain-maker who worked at Villa d'Este. One of his most successful contrivances spurted water from below, drenching the women under their skirts, which 'struck the Signor Cardinal as rather rude', as Vincenzi himself recalls; the Cardinal had it replaced by a 'politer joke which wetted the back upon entering and the face upon leaving', that is to say, 'a trick to wet the bystanders graciously and in gentle fashion' (*Memorandum on Fountains*, 1619).

While the classical garden was one of formal order, in the seventeenth-century garden the viewer was obliged to plunge into greenery, to lose himself in mazes, to get drenched and disport himself, to become an actor on the stage of the baroque garden theatre. In plans of the period it is easy enough to trace the direct influence of designs for stage sets. Already in the previous century the sets of Buontalenti – a brilliant designer of theatrical productions – and of Giulio and Alfonso Parigi, court scenographers, had transformed the classical concept of Florentine Renaissance gardens into scenic phantasmagoria.

'One step further', Mario Praz writes, 'and we shall share, with Andrew Marvell, that rapture of gardens, where things are worshipped in and of themselves; and the worshipping spirit becomes one with nature: "Annihilating all that's made / To a green Thought in a green Shade."'

GEOMETRY AND GRACE

At the end of the seventeenth century a new impulse was given to the art of gardening by the influence of the French style, derived from the lessons of Le Nôtre. New gardening schemes of the period exploited the strict architectural framework that formed the basis of Renaissance gardens, extending linear perspectives, and giving the purity of the geometric parterre a spirit of ornamental elegance borrowed from the sinuous curvilinear forms of French *broderie*. Starting in Piedmont (Le Nôtre very probably did the plan for the royal park of Racconigi near Turin), these free, expressive shapes made their way into nearly every Italian garden, replacing the austerity of traditional classicism with a prestigious new fashion for curves. Perfectly in tune with the conservative spirit of classical Italian gardens, this development was the natural evolution of an historical and above all national tradition, which changed without being revolutionized and was transformed without being destroyed.

THE ROMANTIC SPIRIT

In the eighteenth century the concept of the landscape garden began to take hold in Europe under the influence of the writings of Pope, Addison and Rousseau. One of the first Italian writers to describe the new vogue was Ippolito Pindemonte, in his *Dissertation* dated 1792, but the English landscape style was slow to reach Italy. It did after all represent a complete overthrow of the basic principles governing the plan of the Italian garden. 'Ruled more by sun and marble than by grass and shade', as Pindemonte wrote, Italian gardens did not lend themselves well to landscaping for practical as well as traditional reasons: the Italian climate is too extreme and much of the land too dry for gardens to be landscaped successfully. (In 1904 Edith Wharton was to note that under the scorching summer sun the landscaped gardens of Lombardy, which had by then replaced many of the boxwood parterres, 'turned sable brown'.)

According to the precepts of romanticism, a garden was no longer a formal representation of a sublime and serene intelligence: nor was it a glorification of the power of reason over nature. Gardens became mirrors in which were reflected the emotions, anxieties, dreams and disorders of the romantic soul. In order to evoke the sort of feelings aroused by the landscapes of Poussin, Claude Lorraine and Salvator Rosa, gardening abandoned architecture and sculpture and adopted poetry and painting. It did not seek to create an abstract idea of natural beauty, but set out to imbue gardens with the pastoral gentleness or dramatic grandeur of romantic landscape paintings.

In 1772 Sir William Chambers published his *Dissertation on Oriental Gardening*; he was not the first to examine the philosophy and character of the Chinese garden, but his influence in Europe was profound. Major gardens in France, Germany and England gradually acquired a sprinkling of pavilions, pagodas, tombs and temples in the Chinese style and a spirit of eastern exoticism began to supplant the concept of 'natural' landscapes with an ideal of nature that was not only imaginary but visionary. Chambers argued that the Chinese romantic garden must evoke three categories of emotion – enchantment, surprise and alarm – each one representing an act of an opera or a theatrical production, a view that was appreciated and taken up by Pindemonte. Far from being a liberation of natural forces, the romantic garden choreographed every detail in such a way as to excite the emotions. It relied on the idea that a garden should appear to be an extension of nature but in fact was firmly controlled by strict conventions and disciplines. It came to resemble more and more a great dramatic production in which, as Pindemonte describes, 'marvellous scenes, gentle, pleasant and sublime, suffused with sweet melancholy or depicted with awesome horror', followed one another like stage sets, each one

part of a progression towards a world of sheer fantasy.

Old-established Italian gardens were, however, reluctant to discard their formal grace and elegance for the wilder excesses of romanticism. The landscaping craze was adopted with some enthusiasm in the designing of new gardens, such as those of the Villa Melzi d'Eril in Bellagio, Lombardy, but even then the area nearest to the house generally preserved the conventions of geometrical precision in formal terracing and parterre, while the woods and ponds of a 'natural' landscape were allowed to stretch away into the countryside beyond.

This spirit of compromise and restraint, carefully analysed by the contemporary writer on gardening history, Gianni Venturi, reflects a sensibility that shrank from the extremes of feeling that could be evoked by the romantic garden, seeking to concentrate only on its quieter aspects of gentle enchantment and charm: 'Tranquillity', wrote Ercole Silva in *Dell'arte dei giardini inglesi* (1801; The art of the English garden), 'produces a sweet emotion in the soul, a gentle mood, and a peaceful and lasting delight in its contemplation.'

Even so, the landscaping vogue left its mark on Italy, and very few landowners, unless for lack of funds, failed eventually to change their formal terraces into 'open country in miniature'.

MODERN INSPIRATIONS

As Francis Bacon declared in his celebrated *Essays* of 1625:

God Almighty first planted a garden. And indeed it is the purest of human pleasures. It is the greatest refreshment to the spirits of man; without which, buildings and palaces are but gross handiworks: and a man shall ever see that when ages grow to civility and elegancy, men come to build stately sooner than to garden finely, as if gardening were the greater perfection.

Every great historical and artistic period, from Medici Florence to Baroque Rome and Enlightened Lombardy, has always been accompanied and informed by the creation of magnificent gardens. They are traditional images of power and glory as well as pleasure, but all it takes is a few seasons of neglect for a garden to lose its identity. Statues are damaged; neat boxwood hedges become shapeless; the original plan is swept away by a tide of time and lost, even to memory. To see that this is so one has only to thumb through the indexes of books on Italian gardens written by English, American and German authors at the beginning of this century: more than half the names stir no more than a vague memory, and refer to villas whose gardens are today either unrecognizable or simply no longer in existence.

Partly because of this there is an ever-increasing concern today

with the conservation and restoration of historic gardens, with the aesthetics of their original design, and with the architecture, philosophy, art and poetry that inspired them. A new figure has emerged in the past few decades, the gardener who seeks out the artistic influences that shaped the creation of a garden in order to safeguard or recover its original delicate balance between nature and art.

The British writer and critic Vernon Lee wrote that Italian gardens 'have little or nothing to do with nature'. The observation is paradoxical but true: in the classical Italian garden there were relatively few flowers, and precious botanical collections were almost always kept behind garden walls. Today the situation is very different. While in historic gardens lakes of glistening water may have been designed to bring an image of heaven to earth, the modern garden aims to reproduce a corner of paradise filled with flowers. Humanistic ideals, baroque splendours and romantic dreams, all of which were displayed in gardening terms on a grand and lavish scale, have been replaced in recent years by an appreciation of horticulture and ecology, and gardens are generally arranged in a more intimate and personal way. A garden is no longer, or should no longer be, an opportunity to display the owner's culture, knowledge or wealth, but a setting in which to learn and understand the workings of nature.

REFLECTIONS OF AN IDEAL WORLD

Il Trebbio

Cafaggiolo del Mugello, Tuscany
Virginia & Lorenzo Scaretti

The road from Florence due north to the Futa Pass soon enters the Mugello Valley which extends from the Arno to the Apennines; its gentle rolling hills, punctuated by the thin profiles of cypress trees soaring among the olives, make it one of the most delightful spots in the Florentine countryside. It is this wide view that the eye takes in from the heights of Il Trebbio. In 1451 Cosimo the Elder decided to transform the fourteenth-century fortress into a hunting lodge and engaged the services of Michelozzo di Bartolomei (1396–1472) who had already designed the cloisters of the church of San Marco and the Palazzo Medici-Riccardi in Florence. The strong, square building retained its crenellations and watchtowers, its central courtyard and covered patrol walks, but the garden outside the walls clearly illustrates the gradual shift from a feudal concept of life in the country, in which hunting and jousting were the principal pastimes, to a humanist vision of villa life characterized by more cultural pursuits and quiet reflection.

It was precisely while Il Trebbio was being built that Marsilio Ficino (1433–99) rose to prominence with the founding of the Accademia Platonica in Florence in 1462, first under the patronage of Cosimo de' Medici and then of Lorenzo the Magnificent. A frequently recurring theme in the works of these humanists is the glorification of nature, which was seen as the reflection of a divine

plan, a place of refreshment and meditation inhabited by the shades of divinities. 'The beauty of the flowers', wrote André Chastel, 'and the silence itself, are muses; the voices of the gods ring everywhere in the sky.'

This sense of peace and dedication to divine glory pervades the little fifteenth-century garden to the right of the villa. Consisting of eight square beds of fruit trees, vegetables, aromatic herbs, vines and roses, in structure it is a medieval *hortus conclusus*, or 'garden enclosed', and in spirit a humanist garden. On the left is the old pergola whose columns, built of semicircular red bricks known as *pianelle*, date from the time of Cosimo, and whose vine shades a carpet of grass bordered by miniature climbing roses. Each column has a different capital, in keeping with the Alberti principle of *varietas*, which reflected the Neoplatonic concept of the unity of a single idea expressed in a multiplicity of forms. From the sweet-smelling shade of the pergola the eye takes in a view through the cypresses on the hills beyond the garden. The English writer on Italian gardens and architecture Georgina Masson quite rightly associates this view with the background landscapes of many fifteenth-century depictions of the Annunciation, but it also lends itself to comparison with the description by Eneo Silvio Piccolomini (later Pope Pius II) of the Tuscan landscape which he saw as having

a mystic significance, as if it were itself an expression of religious devotion. The pergola at Il Trebbio therefore has a spiritual meaning which it transmits to the whole garden, confirming its purpose as a place meant not for jousts and games but for contemplation.

The history of Il Trebbio is deeply rooted in the history of Florence as a medieval city state. The children and grandchildren of Cosimo the Elder spent their youthful summers here, and the explorer Amerigo Vespucci (1454–1512) – who gave his name to the American continent – stayed a long time at Trebbio after fleeing from the plague of Florence. Messengers from the Florentine senate came to Trebbio in January 1537 with the news of the assassination of Duke Alessandro de' Medici and the offer to young Cosimo, the future Grand Duke of Tuscany, who was eighteen at the time, of the seigniory of the city.

Owned by the Medicis until 1645, the estate was sold to Giuliano Serragli who bequeathed it to the Oratorio di San Firenze; it was expropriated by the government in 1865. Later it was bought by Prince Marcantonio Borghese, who restored the castle and enhanced the atmosphere of the garden by enclosing it in a sweet-smelling cypress grove. Today the Scaretti family maintain with the greatest care and sensitivity the humanistic spirit of Il Trebbio.

VILLA MEDICI

Castello, Tuscany
Accademia della Crusca

This is the first real example in Italy of a garden created to celebrate the glory and power of its owner – a 'political' garden where every element served one and the same purpose, the glorification of the power of Cosimo de' Medici, the first Grand Duke of Tuscany.

It was by an extraordinary combination of luck, political acumen and military skill that the teenage descendant of a cadet branch of the Medicis came to power in 1537. Cosimo was born at Villa Medici, and one of the first things the new Signore did on inheriting the property was to commission the conversion of the villa and its gardens. The project was entrusted to Nicolò Tribolo in 1538 and was continued after his death by Giorgio Vasari, who made use of the help of Bartolommeo Ammannati and Giambologna. The ideological scheme the garden was designed to illustrate was conceived by

Benedetto Varchi (1503–65), and the main theme, the celebration of Cosimo's power over Tuscany, can still be 'read', despite the great changes carried out in the eighteenth century by the Lorraine dukes, who gave the garden its present-day linear and geometric appearance.

In this original scheme two large fountains represented the two mountains near Florence, Monte Asinaio and Monte Falterona, and the streams of water that issued from them were meant to symbolize the rivers that flowed through Fiesole and Florence, the Mugnone and the Arno. The streams joined to feed the central fountain of the garden which was surmounted by a statue of Venus rising from the waves, the work of Giambologna (it is now in the Villa Medici at Petraia). This system of fountains and watercourses may be said to

page 30 *Villa Medici, today the headquarters of the Accademia della Crusca, a prestigious institute established in the eighteenth century for the study of language, where the celebrated dictionary, the* Vocabolario della Crusca, *is published.*

page 31 *The grotto, with its menagerie of animals sculpted by artists of the school of Giambologna above a stone basin attributed to Ammannati.*

preceding pages *The garden owes its geometric parterre to the work carried out by Pietro Leopoldo di Lorena at the end of the eigtheenth century. Nearly six hundred varieties of citrus fruit are grown in containers symmetrically arranged around the beds.*

above *Winter, a bronze statue by Ammannati that dominates the area around the grotto; together with his statues of Hercules and Antaeus and Giambologna's Venus, it marks the stages of an allegorical route through the garden designed to celebrate the power of Cosimo.*

right *Polychrome stonework and shells on the vaulted roof of the grotto.*

mirror the configuration of the water system of Tuscany, and its orderliness and technical perfection to exalt the good government of Cosimo, which brought strength and prosperity to Florence just as the springs on the hills provided water for the great fountain of Venus.

Linked to this allegorical water system was a grotto, out of which the waters of the hills supposedly spilt; it is connected to the pool where Ammannati's statue of Winter still stands. Concealed within the magnificent grotto is a group of three basins containing bronze and stone sculptures and a collection of shells and fossils representing the natural wonders of the world. An interest in science and a passion for mystery are combined here just as marine, mineral and animal elements are intermingled, melting into the shadows or almost submerged in the water of the fountains. The allegorical key to the menagerie of animals is to be found in the statue of the unicorn at the centre of the middle basin: no longer a mere collection of wonders, the grotto becomes the scene of a mythological fable, that of the unicorn which purifies the water of the fountain poisoned by the serpent by making a sign of the cross in it, thus enabling all animals to quench their thirst. The identification of the unicorn with Cosimo is implicit, while this scene in the grotto is a metaphor for the reforms he introduced and for the peace and harmony he brought to the city state. A statue in front of the villa shows Hercules in the process of strangling the giant Antaeus, surrounded by the splashing waters of a magnificent fountain – the ultimate allegory of the power of the Grand Duke.

Among the relics from the time of the Medicis and the Lorraine dukes is the remarkable collection of about six hundred citrus trees in large terracotta pots, which give the Villa Medici the look of a container garden: oranges, citrons, bergamots, hybrids, and mutants like the horn-shaped orange which combine botanical interest with a touch of the eccentric and bizarre. According to a nineteenth-century description of the garden, the citrus fruits were 'melon-shaped, breast-shaped, cucumber-shaped, plum-, acorn- and pear-shaped and a hundred other figures most strange' – reminiscent of an Arcimboldo fantasy.

VILLA GUARIENTI DI BRENZONE

Lake Garda, Veneto
Conte Guglielmo Guarienti di Brenzone

On the promontory of Punta San Vigilio on the eastern shore of Lake Garda, between Bardolino and Torri del Benaco, stands Villa Guarienti di Brenzone. It was built *c.*1540 by the Mannerist architect Michele Sanmicheli for Agostino Brenzone, who had bought a vast estate in 1538 from the Benedictine monks of San Zeno.

Agostino Brenzone was an important public figure in the Most Serene Venetian Republic. In Venice he had served as a magistrate practising civil and criminal law, but is best remembered as a man of great culture, a friend of the scholar and cardinal Pietro Bembo and the writer Pietro Aretino. A letter exists from the latter, dated 1545, which extols 'the magnificence and the nobility and the excellence of the charming and generous and sublime soul of the broad and fine-looking Agostino Brenzone, grave, just and knowledgeable orator, jurisconsult and philosopher'. This same letter from Aretino refers to the quiet charm of the garden extending from the house to the lake.

Brenzone 'wrote a little work, *Della vita solitaria*, and in order to bring its ideals to reality he built a noble villa with many gardens at San Vigilio on the lake', as Aretino described. The work (the only copy still in the possession of the family was lent to the writer Gabriele D'Annunzio and never returned) echoes back to Petrarch's *De vita solitaria*, with its exhortation to meditate silently in nature. This same desire for tranquillity is reflected in the austere and flawless architecture of the villa and expressed in the layout of the garden: it is a place designed to encourage contemplation, a pure 'garden of the mind', where every element of nature – fruits, trees, stones – summons up classical, literary and mythological recollections. Agostino Brenzone sought not only to design his garden, he 'wrote' it, filling it with Latin inscriptions, poetry and maxims. He displayed a collection of Roman busts in a semicircle of cypress trees, placed a beautiful Greek statue of Venus in the lemon garden and two magnificent bas-reliefs by Girolamo Campagna, one of them of Adam and Eve, among the cypresses. The lemon garden took on,

below Punta San Vigilio, with the villa and the little church on the water's edge. Among the cypresses between them is the Belvedere of the Twelve Caesars, which takes its name from a collection of Roman busts placed here by Agostino Brenzone.

above *Eighteenth-century cypresses clipped into arches screen the garden on the side facing the wide expanses of Lake Garda.*

overleaf *The Greek statue of Venus in the lemon garden. Among the many inscriptions collected by Agostino Brenzone is one which reads, 'Eden brought death, my garden gives life ... Then there was a deceiving serpent, now there is a fatal genius.'*

because of the presence of Venus, a symbolic significance: Pliny had already described lemons as a combination of sweet and bitter, paving the way for the metaphorical identification of lemons with love, of which Venus is the goddess. An inscription underlines the garden's association with love: 'Fruits sweet and bitter grow, frozen and fiery; so love grows in our heart.'

In the eighteenth century the Guarienti di Brenzone family planted the arched cypress hedges that link the older parts of the garden. The entire estate has remained in their hands until the present day. They have defended the property from alterations of any kind, resisting all landscaping fashions and all temptations, however economically justified, to replace the fantastic labyrinth of hedges with features that were easier to maintain. The lake has an atmosphere of peace and quiet that has remained almost unchanged

through the centuries, and that it transmits to the whole garden.

Guarienti di Brenzone's garden is contemporary with the great Roman Renaissance gardens, but its style is completely alien to them. In spite of its dimensions, the impression it creates is not one of sheer size but rather of austerity and restraint. It is not a worldly place but a spiritual retreat, a refuge intended for contemplation. It was Agostino Brenzone himself who laid down the laws for his guests in an inscription placed beneath his marble bust: 'Banish the toils of city life. Dismiss women from thy sight and all that concerns them. Lay thy table without luxury. Nourish thy soul with the love of things. Accept fronds, flowers and fruit in great abundance ...'

This is far indeed from Renaissance hedonism. The spirit of this humanistic garden was dominated by the severity of a strict education – cultured, moral and rigorous.

ART, ARTIFICE AND NATURE

VILLA IMPERIALE

Pesaro, Marche
Conti Castelbarco Albani

Nephew of Julius II, heir to Guidobaldo da Montefeltro, Francesco Maria della Rovere became Duke of Urbino in 1508. The duchy, secluded in the hills of the Marche, became the centre of a magnificent court of which the leading spirits were Baldassare Castiglione (author of *The Courtier*), Pietro Bembo and Girolamo Genga. Its harmony was destroyed with the accession of Leo X, who forced the duke into exile to oblige Lorenzo de' Medici, but on the death of the Pope in 1521, Francesco Maria was able to return for good to Urbino and Pesaro (which had been annexed to the duchy in 1512). And in order to celebrate the new-found peace and the consolidation of the duchy, and to express her devotion to Francesco Maria, his wife Eleonora Gonzaga started work on the construction of the villa and its gardens. An inscription, composed by Cardinal Bembo, on the façade of the building reads:

For Francesco Maria, Duke of the Metaurian States on his return from the wars, his consort Eleonora has erected this villa in token of affection, and in compensation for sun and dust, for watching and toil, so that during an interval of repose his military genius may prepare for him still wider renown and richer rewards.

The villa lies just to the west of Pesaro on the slope of Mount San Bartolo, facing the valley of the Foglia river. The site had been chosen in 1468 by Alessandro Sforza, at that time Signore of Pesaro, for the building of a massive turreted palace. Emperor Frederick III was present for the laying of the cornerstone, and the memory of that visit is preserved in the name of the villa.

Around 1523 Eleonora Gonzaga commissioned Girolamo Genga to make a number of alterations to the original building; his work included the design of an extension in which the military austerity of the Sforza palace gave way to the grandeur of a Renaissance villa. Genga had been a painter in the studios of Signorelli and Perugino and, a friend of Raphael, had been able in Rome to follow his work on Villa Madama and to visit the gardens of Bramante's Belvedere created for Julius II. Thus it was through him that the provincial duchy of Urbino was introduced into the mainstream of Renaissance architecture.

The fifteenth-century Sforza palace was converted into living quarters, and the new building, free of all practical obligations, became a pure stage set, designed exclusively for the summer seasons of a court that spent its time in the pursuit of pleasure, in playing games, reading, and devising plots, both real and literary. The villa is situated on a steep slope, at the bottom of which stands the original main building. The entrance is approached by way of an enclosed space supported by high arches that recall the Basilica of Maxentius in Rome and that leads into a courtyard surrounded by high walls. There is no view to help the visitor solve the quandary of finding himself in a place from which there is apparently no way out.

Opposite the portico is a passageway, but it leads to a grotto. Looking up, one can see balustrades and loggias on top of the walls, but they reveal nothing, merely suggesting the layout of the Renaissance villa on various upper storeys. Only by means of stairs hidden inside a wall does one reach the second level, which is taken up by a lovely hanging garden overlooking the courtyard. From here another staircase leads to the top storey of the villa where, divided into regular geometric flowerbeds, a perfect Italian garden stretches ahead. Looking back from the far end, one can see nothing but the garden itself and the long terraces which mask the roof all the way round the building. With a cunning theatrical touch, the main body of the new building has disappeared again, and the garden seems to be bordered only by the open sky. The courtyard hides the gardens which in turn hide the villa, a highly effective dramatic device by which all the mechanics of the architecture are completely concealed, in keeping with the precepts of Castiglione: 'One can say that real art is what does not seem to be art; nor should aught be studied but to conceal it.' In 1538 one of the Duke's administrators wrote that the villa and the gardens were 'truly now a place to be enjoyed with pleasure'.

The first hanging garden was planted with espaliered lemon trees, whereas the second, much larger one was given over to varieties of myrtle, vines, and pots of orange and lemon trees set among roses and beds of rosemary. Visitors of the time remembered box hedges shaped like boats, though no trace of them remains. The Renaissance spirit of these gardens lies in their being laid out and decorated like rooms, enclosed by high walls that separate them from the surrounding woods and protect them from the wind. They are, in fact, the perfect reflection of a magnificent court life which flourished in seclusion, suspended in a universe outside time and history and far removed from dust and wars, as the Villa Imperiale was.

With the extinction of the della Rovere dukes the villa passed to the Medicis and then to the Lorraines. In 1763 it became the property of the Apostolic Camera which assigned it to the Jesuits driven out of Portugal, and at the end of the eighteenth century it came into the possession of the Albani counts. During the nineteenth century it gradually fell into decay and was seriously damaged by shelling during the Second World War. Meticulous restoration work was, however, undertaken by Count Guglielmo Castelbarco Albani, who thus gave back to the Marche its most beautiful Renaissance garden.

opposite *The main courtyard of the villa. The design of the arched entrance was probably suggested to its architect, Girolamo Genga, by the Roman basilica of Maxentius.*

Villa Cicogna Mozzoni

Bisúschio, Lombardy
Contessa Eleonora Cicogna Mozzoni

There is no country house in Lombardy that reflects the genius of Renaissance architecture more than does Villa Cicogna Mozzoni, where interior and exterior spaces blend into a graceful, co-ordinated whole. Rather than the garden borrowing its layout from the house, it is the building which seems to throw itself open to the magnificent views outside, creating a perfect balance between garden and villa.

The house stands on a rise facing the foothills of the Viggiù Alps near Varese. It was not conceived as a single plan, and the names of the architects who worked here are unknown: only the principal stages in the development of the property over the years have been recorded. In the fourteenth century the noble Mozzoni family owned a hunting lodge at Bisúschio. In 1476, according to chronicles of the time, Galeazzo Maria Sforza, Duke of Milan, was staying as a guest of the Mozzonis and was attacked by a bear while out with a hunting party; he was courageously saved by Agostino Mozzoni and his dogs, and from that moment on the fortunes of the family took a decided turn for the better. The Bisúschio house was converted and greatly enlarged between 1530 and 1560 by Ascanio Mozzoni who gave it its Renaissance aspect. In 1580 his only child, Angiola, married Giovanni Pietro Cicogna, and their line has continued uninterruptedly to the present owners.

The garden, the central part of which has remained intact, was set out around 1560 by the same Ascanio Mozzoni, a man of culture who in his travels to Florence and Rome absorbed the new architectural ideas of the day, which were then being developed in the Medici and papal villas. The two arms of the U-shaped Villa Cicogna Mozzoni open out on to a flawless formal garden enclosed at the end by a wall of porous stone (probably inspired by the grottos of the Villa Medici at Castello in Florence) which is hollowed into niches filled with statuary. Balustrading extends along the top of the wall and also encloses two rectangular pools at ground level. The wall is the same height as the ground floor of the house, with the result that the garden appears to be an extension of the villa, like a magnificent open-air living room furnished with statues and fountains. The

preceding page *A view from above which shows the enclosed parterre at Villa Cicogna Mozzoni and the symmetry of its sixteenth-century design.*

below *The lower part of the rill that descends to the fountain at the foot of the great water staircase.*

right *The arcaded loggia frescoed by the Campi brothers with a curvilinear design of figures, fruit and flowers.*

ground floor of the two arms of the villa consists of arcaded loggias, their ceilings frescoed with floral motifs, garlands and vine branches, linking the outer and inner spaces and letting the light of the garden into the halls and reception rooms. The frescoes, the work of Giulio, Antonio and Vincenzo Campi of Cremona and their school, were painted not long before 1560 (according to Giacomo Bascapé, a contemporary historian) and perform a strictly architectural function of transition: the portico space belongs in volume to the building but in decoration and colour to the garden. Its frescoes recall those of Giovanni da Udine in the Farnesina in Rome, where gardening combines seamlessly with architecture through the medium of painting.

Following the slope of the hill, which rises beyond the wall at the end of the Renaissance garden, is one of the most celebrated water staircases of the sixteenth century: a double row of cypress trees guides the eye from a portico at the top, and down two parallel flights of stone steps between which a stream of water flows, spilling into a fountain set on a level with the windows of the great hall on the second floor of the villa.

A large terrace laid out in traditional Italian style provides a physical and visual link between the water staircase and a terraced garden on the other side of the house, looking towards Lake Lugano. It also offers a sheltered place in which to walk and enjoy the views of the parterre and surrounding landscape.

The Villa Cicogna Mozzoni and its garden owe much to the great Renaissance architecture of Rome, but in the grandeur and stateliness of its vistas it places more emphasis on elegance than on pageantry and more on serenity and restraint than on opulent display.

right The balustraded wall of porous stone, ornamented with niches and statuary, that encloses the Italian garden and provides a theatrical backcloth to its formal parterre.

Villa Lante Della Rovere

Bagnaia, Lazio

'Then with the Pope remounted on horseback in a tempest of men, harquebusiers, trumpets, drums and bells, we reached Bagnaia. The Pope's lodging was splendid and royal and that of the cardinal magnificent beyond words.' Thus begins the chronicle of the journey made by Clement VIII in 1598 to the villa at Bagnaia, summer residence of the Bishop of Viterbo, an important see because of its closeness to Rome, and for that reason almost always occupied by a powerful cardinal 'nephew' of the Pope. In 1550 there was only a park and a hunting lodge here, built by Cardinal Riario, a place that could hardly hope to satisfy the ambition, culture and wealth of Giovanni Francesco Gambara, who was made a cardinal at the age of twenty-eight by Pius IV Medici and became Bishop of Viterbo in 1566.

Work started around 1568, entrusted in all probability to Giacomo da Vignola (1507–73) who had already designed the Villa Farnese at Caprarola, Viterbo, and it resulted in the most perfect and complete example of an Italian Renaissance garden. Only one visitor failed to share the general enthusiasm it excited, and did not hide his disappointment: San Carlo Borromeo who, according to a biography of 1613 mentioned by the historian Angelo Cantoni, 'was received by Cardinal Gambara, who showed him over those enchanting gardens, but he, being of a different mind, never answered him, and as Gambara went on questioning him, he finally replied, saying, "Monsignore, you would have done better to build a Nunnery with the money you have thrown away constructing this place".'

In 1590 it become the property of Cardinal Alessandro Montalto, the nephew of Sixtus V, who completed the garden. The estate later passed to the Ludovisi, Barberini and Sforza families. In 1656 it was rented in perpetuity to Duke Ippolito Lante della Rovere in exchange for property he owned in Rome, and the villa, the garden and its fountains remained in the family for three hundred years. Today Villa Lante belongs to the state and its upkeep is exemplary.

The garden is laid out along a watercourse which descends in stages from the top of the garden, passing through a series of fountains and finally widening into a number of large pools. In order to retain an uninterrupted perspective it was decided not to build a villa as such but two small symmetrical pavilions instead: Gambara was responsible for one and Montalto for the other. They form part of an integrated whole in which a perfect balance is established between the volumes of the buildings, the lines of the garden and the rhythmic sequence of the fountains.

The drop of about fifty feet from the top of the garden to the bottom is divided into five embankments forming terraces which are occupied by fountains of increasing size, connected in such a way that the perspective plan of the garden can be taken in at a single glance from the main entrance below. The uncompromising order and logic of this scheme is tempered by the free movement of rushing, arching, cascading water, which pours like rain out of the Fountain of the Flood set in a grotto at the top of the garden, falls into the Fountain of the Dolphins, and flows into a magnificent chain of pools shaped like crayfish, a play on Cardinal Gambara's name (the Italian word for crayfish is *gambero*) before pouring into the great Fountain of the Giants. From here it slips into the channel that runs the length of the cardinal's dining table, passes into an underground pipeline and re-emerges in the seventy vertical jets of the Fountain of the Lamplights, which looks like an enormous candlestick with silver flames; it ends its long journey in the great square parterre of water surrounding the magnificent Fountain of the Moors, in the centre of which are the arms of Cardinal Montalto.

A symbolic meaning can be read into this sequence of fountains: the water's gradual passage from the surging Fountain of the Flood to the serene pools of the Fountain of the Moors marks and celebrates the dominance of reason over the forces of nature, and, as the writer David Coffin has suggested, it represents the progression through the golden age to the ideals and philosophy of the Renaissance. Natural forces ordered and controlled by man: this is the strict dialectic of the Renaissance garden, which at Bagnaia is expressed in the contrast between the vagaries of the water in the upper fountains and the restraint and calm of the lower ones, as well as between the sunny aspect of the garden proper and the great shady park surrounding it.

THE SACRED GROVE OF BOMARZO

Viterbo, Lazio
Giovanni Bettini

'You who go wandering about the world in search of sublime and awesome wonders, come here where horrendous faces, elephants, lions, bears, ogres and dragons are to be seen.' This is the invitation, carved in stone, to enter the most fantastic sixteenth-century garden in Europe, the Sacro Bosco, or Sacred Grove, which Pier Francesco 'Vicino' Orsini (1513–84) created at Bomarzo. The name 'Sacred Grove' probably derives from the fact that there was once a chapel here dedicated to the memory of Giulia Farnese, the wife of Orsini. The gardens themselves were laid out, as he himself wrote, 'to satisfy the heart' – and to amuse himself and entertain and astonish others.

In 1949 Salvador Dali drew attention to the ruins of a world of monsters buried under a mass of undergrowth in the region of Monti Cimini, north-west of Rome, an area famous for its grand villas. It is hard to say what the place must have looked like originally. From the castle of Bomarzo a path may have led through a large formal garden, which no longer exists; and at the far end it crossed a stone bridge into the valley of the grove, where the serenity of the park gave way to monstrous figures carved out of the tufa rocks scattered about the grounds.

'Of venerable aspect', so Francesco Sansovino describes Vicino Orsini, 'he loved arms but letters even more.' Orsini took part in various military campaigns, returning from prison in Flanders in 1558 to his father's castle in Bomarzo, which he converted into a palace. A patron of the arts, and a poet himself, he was on good terms with Annibale Caro, Claudio Tolomei and Francesco Sansovino; he was a friend of Bernardo Tasso and Molza, as well as the powerful Cardinal Madruzzo who was instrumental in organizing the Council of Trent. Several letters still in existence offer clues to his tastes and inclinations; an eclectic figure, he was irresistibly drawn to the eccentric and bizarre; he loved to read Rabelais, sought out books about the East Indies and discourses on longevity, he disdained philosophers and enthused about romantic epic poetry. It is unquestionably this rich mixture of literacy influences that inspired the figures in the garden. The original intention may have been to carve in stone scenes from *L'Adamigi di Gaula* and *Il Floridante*, chivalric epics by Bernardo Tasso, the father of the poet Torquato, recreating the enchanted forest strewn with obstacles which the

right, overleaf and pages 58–9 *The awe-inspiring world of real and mythical beasts that inhabit the Sacred Grove created by Vicino Orsini in the sixteenth century.*

knight had to overcome in order to win his beloved. But the stone dragons and the huge tortoise recall the fabulous oriental sculptures described by the Jesuits Paul III sent to India; the giant figures are those to be found in the Pantagruelian universe of Rabelais; the gloomy caves gaping in the woods evoke the world of the Etruscans; and the colossus tearing the woman asunder may represent an episode from Ludovico Ariosto's epic *Orlando Furioso* (1532).

Though the individual images of the Sacred Grove, 'extravagant and supernatural things', as Annibale Caro called them, can be traced back to the literature of the period, their introduction into the art of gardening is unique. In fact Bomarzo represents a spectacular and revolutionary departure from the laws governing the design of the Renaissance garden (of which magnificent examples can be seen nearby, at Caprarola and Bagnaia). Linear clarity and perspective views do not exist here. As a result of their natural spacing, the great rocks from which the monsters were carved do not follow a

symmetrical plan in accordance with the normal formula. And every rule of proportion has been subverted in the carving of these creatures, just as the principle of realism has been completely abandoned in favour of effects calculated purely to amaze. The visitor is no longer offered reassuring views from on high: to see the garden he has to enter it and, as an inscription at Bomarzo says, 'with arched brows and tightened lips', knowing nothing of what awaits him, set off on a journey through a natural landscape inhabited by massive and often alarming figures.

The garden is not intended as a celebration of human genius, or of man's culture and power, but as a place where nature is exalted and the imagination is free to roam. Turning its back on the orderliness of abstract geometry and the security of a world centred on man, the Renaissance spirit gradually draws towards the great mystery of nature and plunges into an unknown universe, just as Vicino Orsini lost himself in literary fantasies and as the visitor to Bomarzo wanders at will in the garden he created.

RUSPOLI CASTLE

Vignanello, Lazio
Principe Alessandro Ruspoli

Set in a great rectangular space between two screens of holm oaks, crossed by four straight alleys and divided into twelve parterres with trimmed box hedges, the garden of the Ruspoli palace has the clarity of a geometrical formula.

The castle was transformed in 1574, and although by then the need for defences had greatly diminished and the military power of the wealthy Roman feudal families had considerably declined, it preserves all the characteristic features of a stronghold, with its fortified towers and bastions, its four-square ground plan and its sentry walk protected by Guelph battlements. Power and family prestige, explicit in the architecture of the castle, are implicit in the design of the garden. The magnificent box hedges of the parterres trace the initials of Ottavia Orsini and her sons, Sforza and Galeazzo: the monograms seem to set their seal not only on the gardens but also on the surrounding territory. The sense of order and precision that prevailed in the running of the Ruspoli family estates is reflected in the long, straight perspectives of the garden's avenues.

Vignanello, formerly the fief of Cesare Borgia and the Farnese dynasty, became in 1536 the property of the Marescotti family, one of whose descendants inherited the estate in 1704 with the obligation of taking on the Ruspoli name. Still today the summer residence of the Ruspoli princes, the castle has changed little since alterations were carried out in about 1610 by Ottavia Orsini, the wife of Marc'Antonio Marescotti and the daughter of Vicino Orsini, the creator of the nearby garden of Bomarzo, whose mysterious character is the nocturnal reverse of the severe Late Renaissance classicism of the Ruspoli garden.

below and right Trim box hedges laid out with formal precision around the castle of the Ruspoli princes.

VILLA ALDOBRANDINI

Frascati, Lazio
Principe & Principessa Aldobrandini

Villa Aldobrandini is the finest example of the grandeur and magnificence attained by the papal court at the end of the sixteenth century. As with all the villas of Frascati, Aldobrandini's position – on a hillside sloping towards Rome – is magnificent, and of all of them it is the one whose character, decoration and gardens are best preserved today. The villa passed to the powerful Roman family of Pamphili in 1683 and to the Borgheses in 1760. It returned to the Aldobrandini family through an inheritance in 1843.

The revenues and temporal power of Pope Clement VIII were greatly increased by the addition of Ferrara to the Papal States in 1598, an event which owed much to the diplomatic skills of his nephew Pietro Aldobrandini. From that day on the young man's fortunes were to prosper in a remarkable way. In 1598 he received an estate and a small house known as the Villa del Belvedere, dating from about 1560, as a present from the Apostolic Camera. This villa was incorporated into a much more imposing building designed by Giacomo della Porta (1532/3–1602), who was also commissioned to lay out an initial scheme for the garden, which was completed in 1603, a year after his death. Domenico Fontana and Carlo Maderno were subsequently engaged to carry out enlargements and recon-structions, which were finished around 1620. They also designed the great cascade and the magnificent Water Theatre behind the villa.

The entire building, and the layout of the surrounding grounds, pursued a single aim: to create a tangible image dedicated to the glory of the Pope and the power of his cardinal nephew. Pietro Aldobrandini also purchased the nearby and loftier Villa La Ruffinella for the reasons which he himself explained: 'That both from the front and from the sides, from the south and from the east, there be no one who commands or looks into my property; on the contrary that from all places I be the higher as I am now.'

To this end Villa Aldobrandini was designed to afford views taking in the whole horizon, which was thereby identified with the boundary of an ideal property that embraced the world, just as the power of the Church encompassed the universe. In a report on the villa written by Cardinal Pietro's secretary, Giovanni Battista Agucchi, for Charles Emmanuel II of Savoy, this 'political vista' was described as follows: 'To the front one descries the city of Rome and its countryside, between west and south the sea; about the countryside castles, estates, towns and all that is to be found in a most grand and most vast country seems to make room and adornment for this house.' In other words, the universe and Villa Aldobrandini were simply one and the same.

preceding pages: left *Villa Aldobrandini from the top of the water staircase;*
right *The pillars of Hercules, representing the power of human
knowledge and wisdom, flank the steps that carry 'the waters from Monte Algido'
to the fountains below.*

below *At the centre of the magnificent Water Theatre stands a figure of
Atlas holding a globe on his shoulders, an allegory of the dominion of Clement VIII
who held the fate of the Church in his hands.*

right *The statue of Pan, one of the sylvan gods in niches around
the Water Theatre.*

But the great house and its garden represented not only the universal scope of Christianity but the force of an infinite power over all things, over men and nature. It is the attainment of this power which is celebrated in the last part of a 118-metre inscription carved on a frieze in the Water Theatre: 'Cardinal Pietro ... transported here the waters from Monte Algido.' This was indeed an achievement worthy of glory – the creation of a garden in which fountains, cascades and waterworks abound, in a place as dry and barren as Frascati. To supply water to the garden the hydraulic system of the entire area was disrupted, and the task took on the significance of a challenge to nature, a gauge of the power of the Aldobrandini dynasty. This astonishingly ambitious endeavour resulted in the imposing spectacle of a water staircase carrying a stream from the top of the hill into the fountains of the nymphaeum. 'The effects which the water creates in its descent', Agucchi writes, 'are so beautiful it can be said to run, to fall, to rush, to leap and dance, to draw back, to gush through tunnels, to bubble and boil and

a thousand other things simultaneously.'

This is the centrepiece of the garden, and it draws upon both history and mythology in its glorification of the papal family. The concept, form and dimensions of the Water Theatre refer back to the most celebrated models of antiquity, such as the nymphaea of Domitian and Hadrian's Villa in Tivoli and, in more recent times, Raphael's Villa Madama in Rome (1516–20). The statues of Polyphemus and the Centaur, which adorn the niches of the semicircular wall, are borrowed from classical mythology, while the central figure of the giant holding aloft a globe is all that remains of a group that once showed Atlas supporting the heavens with the help of Hercules. The identification of Atlas with Clement VIII and Hercules with Pietro Aldobrandini is clear, and is stressed by the two huge spiral pillars that flank the steps at the top of the cascade; towering over the nymphaeum, they represent the Pillars of Hercules, symbols of knowledge and power extending to the ends of the earth.

Palazzo Corsini

Florence, Tuscany
Principe & Principessa Corsini

In 1621 Marchese Filippo Corsini, as a document of the period reports, bought from the Acciaiuoli family 'a large house, begun but not finished', just outside the Porta al Prato in Florence, near the celebrated Oricellari Gardens where the Accademia Platonica met. The purchase of the building was a reflection of the economic and political fortune that shone on the Corsini family at the time and was to do so increasingly in the future, with Lorenzo Corsini ascending the throne of St Peter's in 1730 under the name of Clement XII.

The construction of the palace had been largely entrusted to Bernardo Buontalenti, and was finished by Gherardo Silvani. His son was to build the Via di Parione palace in Florence, also for the Corsinis, which for many years became the main family residence: until 1834 the Porta al Prato palazzo was merely a 'place of pleasure' in which to enjoy a few hours in the quiet and shade of the garden, and perhaps to escape that 'monotony of peace and plenty' which Henry James felt in the Via di Parione rooms.

The central and most important feature of the palazzo is the magnificent loggia at the back. Designed by Buontalenti and built three feet above ground level, it dominates the garden, acting as a light and graceful link between the external spaces and the architecture of the villa.

The garden, probably the work of Silvani himself, is conceived entirely in terms of the loggia and its roof terrace, which is not so much for the pleasure of taking strolls as for viewing the garden from above. It is, in fact, from the terrace that the pattern created by the beds of trimmed boxwood in the garden can best be seen. Their geometrical symmetry is a perfect reflection of the Renaissance spirit, far removed from the *broderie* flourishes of French flower-beds. The garden is divided into two parts by a central avenue running from the loggia: this straight line is accentuated by a succession of Roman statues standing on bases of diminishing size, a device which enhances the perspective effect of the avenue.

The classical spirit that pervades historic Italian gardens, evoking the splendours of the patrician villas of Rome, is still to be found in the loggia of the Palazzo Corsini garden: it is ornamented with a lavish collection of marbles and engraved inscriptions discovered in Rome in 1673.

Two wooded groves were planted on either side of the garden in the nineteenth century, but the only change to have occurred here in recent times was the happy inspiration of its present owner Donna Giorgiana Corsini, who filled the boxwood beds beneath the lemon trees with lavender, whose scent mingles with the fragrance of roses blooming in front of the loggia.

right The garden seen from the loggia behind the palazzo; overleaf The symmetrical boxwood parterre.

DRAMA AND DELIGHT

VILLA DI CETINALE

Ancaiano, Tuscany
Lord Lambton

'Whoever you are who comes here, what to you may seem ugly to me seems beautiful. If it pleases you remain, if not depart. I shall anyway be thankful.' This is the inscription in Latin, carved on a marble slab in an outdoor gallery, which welcomes guests to Villa di Cetinale near Siena. The hospitality it expresses accurately reflects the character of the villa itself, which was never a showplace but the house which the Chigis, who were Sienese bankers, bishops and administrators, lived in for short stays in the country. The building can be seen today just as it appears in a late seventeenth-century drawing in the Vatican Library. It was built a little before 1680 for Flavio Cardinal Chigi, nephew of Alexander VII, by Carlo Fontana (1634–1714), a pupil of Bernini, and his work is one of the rare expressions of Roman baroque architecture in Tuscany.

Flavio Chigi was one of the last great Roman cardinals to be appointed as a direct result of being a nephew of the Pope – a year before his death in 1693, Pope Innocent XII put an end to all such nepotism (the very word derives from the Italian word *nipote*, meaning nephew) – but Alexander VII followed the old tradition: he arranged for his nephew to be ordained priest and appointed him cardinal ten months later at the early age of twenty-six.

Flavio Chigi's gifts were probably more political and diplomatic than spiritual, and his culture was imbued with the spirit of eclecticism which distinguished his century. In his house on Via Quattro Fontane in Rome he assembled a fantastic collection of oddities and curiosities: Turkish weapons, stuffed birds, fossils, minerals, corals, erotic statuettes, trinkets, Egyptian papyrus scrolls and, as can be read in a 1706 inventory, 'a Turk's nose, mouth and moustache'. Surrounding this museum of marvels was a garden, no longer in existence. It too was designed by Carlo Fontana, and in it the passion for the strange and mysterious, which was given free rein in the collection, was combined with a sense of ascetic spiritualism: 'In the upper part', a contemporary description of the garden reports, 'there is a Hermitage which teaches moderation in the delights of this world.'

opposite *The entrance front of Villa Cetinale, the work of Carlo Fontana.*

overleaf *Above the windows on the first floor of the rear façade are the arms of the Chigi family, surmounted by the tiara of Alessandro VII, the cardinal's hat of Flavio Chigi and the crown of the marquisate.*

Delights, and moderation in their enjoyment, were the basis and inspiration for Fontana's design for the Chigi garden at Cetinale. In front of the main façade of the villa is a formal Italian garden adorned with statues by Mazzuoli, and from a flight of steps at the back a broad straight avenue leads to the original entrance to the villa, a great gateway flanked by two gigantic statues. The line of this avenue crosses a semicircular theatre, continues on its way in the form of a long, steep flight of steps and climbs up through woods to a hermitage, a link with the Chigi house in Rome. This small building, with a large cross carved on its façade, dominates the surrounding landscape.

The hermitage is set on an axis with the villa, and the perfectly straight line that cuts through the fields and woods from one building to the other creates a perspective that is both dramatic in its effect and symbolic in its significance. Guiding the eye from the villa to the cross on the hermitage, it seems to be the physical representation of a spiritual call, distracting attention from the delights of worldly possessions and beckoning one on to contemplation and prayer. Its symbolism is underlined by the numerous statues of hermits and the votive chapels which line the path through the woods. This route, which the visitor takes to reach the villa, is the so-called Thebaid of Cetinale; it passes through a 'sacred grove' whose silence and shadows provide a spiritual atmosphere for these ancient statues, whose faces have been eroded over the centuries. Natural and contrived effects contribute in equal measure to the glorification of an ideal which is as much pure theatre as a moral dialectic.

Cardinal Flavio left the villa to his Chigi Zondadari nephews, whose descendants retained it for almost three hundred years. Then in 1977 it was bought by its present owner, Anthony Lambton. Having retired from parliament in England, he used to spend his summers in a farmhouse near Cetinale, and from there he could see the gradual deterioration of the villa. He decided to rescue it, and undertook a major programme of restoration, recapturing in the process some of the original air of propriety that had once filled this cardinal's house and reviving the spirit of hospitality expressed by the welcoming Latin inscription.

Part of the old garden, protected by an embankment round the house, was converted by Claire Ward into an enchanting *giardino segreto* (or secret garden): neat beds are divided by pergolas on which grow *Rosa* 'Alberic Barbier', *R.* 'Constance Spry' and *R.* 'Mme Plantier' mixed with yellow jasmine. In spite of the words of the seventeenth-century commentator, no sense of 'moderation' seems to restrain its 'delight'.

above and right The ancient walls of the 'secret garden' are covered with a mixture of climbing roses, pinks, rosemary and valerian.

Borromean Islands

Lake Maggiore, Piedmont
Principe & Principessa Borromeo

Whenever the poetic imagination has wanted to give visible form to the concept of an idealized nature it has portrayed it as an island garden: the physical isolation of an island and the enclosed privacy of a garden combine to create an image in which the seclusion and otherworldliness of each are intensified. The Hesperides hid the tree of the golden apples in an island garden, and on the island of Ogygia Calypso detained Ulysses for seven years. These examples were certainly not unknown to Count Carlo Borromeo when in *c.* 1630 he undertook the creation of the splendid gardens of Isola Bella in honour of his wife Isabella d'Adda, after whom the place was named. In character the island seems closer to the mythical hanging gardens of Babylon than to the shores of Lake Maggiore.

'The Borromean Islands', wrote Bishop Burnet of Salisbury in 1685, 'are certainly the most beautiful stretches of land in this world'; 'the Eden of Italy', John Ruskin called them, supported with an extravagance verging on hyperbole by Stendhal who described this as 'one of the most beautiful places in the world' and Lake Maggiore itself as 'one of the most beautiful lakes in the universe'. Isola Bella is unquestionably the island of hyperbole, in its gardens and design no less than in the things that have been written about it.

The creation of the palazzo and gardens of Isola Bella was a Promethean achievement. At the beginning of the seventeenth century the island was little more than a clay rock. The work undertaken by Count Carlo Borromeo, together with the architect

preceding pages *The great baroque palace, now a museum, occupies one end of the island transformed by Count Carlo Borromeo in honour of his wife, Isabella d'Adda. A village has sprung up around the church to the right of it, and the gardens extend the length of the far shore.*

these pages *The great gardens of Isola Bella, laid out in ten terraces and ornamented with statuary, grottoes, arcaded passageways and exotic planting, are a magnificent example of the seventeenth-century taste for opulence and display; far left, below The garden theatre, a detail of which can be seen above, is crowned with the Borromeo unicorn and the family motto, 'Humilitas'.*

Angelo Crivelli, involved not so much the transformation of the natural features of the place as their total substitution: 'As much rock as was destroyed', De Vit recalls, 'as much again was used to build pillars, arches and walls, and as much earth was brought from the mainland' as was required to make a garden. The concept of human excellence was reflected in the realization of a plan to turn a barren island into the most extravagant of baroque stage sets, representing the triumph of human genius, and the power of the house of Borromeo in particular, over nature.

The works were finished in 1670 by Count Vitaliano Borromeo, the son of Count Carlo, and its appearance has remained almost unaltered to the present day. The design, in which plants, pillars and statues are given equal importance, is based on the balance and interplay between spaces, slopes, staircases, balustrades and archways; the components of this magnificent structure look like the joints and ribbings of a great ship afloat on the water.

The arrangement of the terraces was conceived purely in terms of theatrical effect, and during the Borromeos' sojourns on the lake the island actually became a spectacular floating theatre. In 1666 music

above and right *Isola Madre was originally known as Isola di San Vittore and later as Isola Renata in honour of Renato Borromeo, who completed work on the villa at the beginning of the seventeenth century.*

above *The famous white peacocks of Isola Madre. Azaleas, rhododendrons, camellias and magnolias grow in profusion on the island, as they have done since the eighteenth century.*

right *The approach to the Borromeo villa on Isola Madre.*

was written for choruses hidden in the garden; in the evening singers were carried by boat along the terraced shores while a performance of *L'Ipocondria scacciata dall'isola dell'Allegrezza'* (Hypochondria driven from the Island of Merriment) was given in the little theatre, which no longer exists. It was this same Arcadian enchantment that was described in a report of a visit by the widow of Charles II of Spain in June 1708: 'In the evening sweet symphonies and musical serenades pleasing to the ear were heard, witty fires of merriment flying everywhere.'

This ornamental masterpiece, where very little is left to nature or imagination, was described by the nineteenth-century English painter Brockedon as an island 'worthy of the extravagance of a rich man with the taste of a confectioner', while Wordsworth's sister exclaimed in 1820, both appalled and amazed: 'The peak of absurdity, a garden not of flowers but of stones, where coloured pebbles take the place of flowers.' All these visitors had to do, however, was to steer their vessels across the lake to discover the

most romantic of island gardens, it too owned by the Borromeo family.

Isola Madre was rented in 1502 on a long-term lease to Count Lancellotto Borromeo who started work on the palazzo and its garden. His plans were carried forward by Count Renato who bought the island in 1600. There were, and still are, no marble statues or theatres; instead a small classical Italian garden lies in front of the villa, but terraces planted with spectacular rhododendrons and semi-tropical trees give the place an even greater luxuriance than Isola Bella. A 1542 survey lists some of the things grown there then – 'vines, walnuts, figs, olives, cherries, jujubes, morellos'. Such was the oriental allure of this Piedmontese island that Flaubert in 1845 thought he could see 'a grave and gentle sultan appear from behind a bush with his precious yataghan and silk robe'. Isola Madre has never lost its original character, although it has been embellished over the centuries by exotic touches like the white peacocks for which it is famous.

VILLA BARBARIGO

Valsanzibio, Veneto
Conte Fabio Pizzoni Ardemani

In a letter dated 10 August 1539 astronomer Andrea Piccolomini wrote:

I came to a Villa a little over ten miles from Padua called Valsanzibio, a most lovely place, delectable not so much for the sweetness of the air, which is most perfect, as for every other gift of nature one usually desires in a villa, like crystal-clear waters, where various comforts may be had all day in laying traps and conspiracies against Fish and Birds.

And it was the sweetness of this scenery which in 1669 persuaded the Procurator of the Venetian Republic, Antonio Barbarigo, brother of the Blessed Gregory, to convert a family estate in the Euganean hills into what is still today the most beautiful seventeenth-century garden in the Veneto.

Antonio Barbarigo decided to replace the simple pleasures described by Piccolomini with more sophisticated and elegant delights. Groups of statues and fountains were laid out, each with an inscription, often enigmatic and allusive in form, referring to mythology, history and morals and lending the garden an allegorical and Arcadian quality. An inscription on the staircase leading to the villa reads: 'Here a brighter Sun shines its rays; here a more beautiful Venus rises from the sea; here the phases of the Moon are more luminous; here Jove plays calmly and his face is serene.'

preceding pages Villa Barbarigo and its formal garden against a background of the Euganean hills.

below and right The remarkable edifice known as 'Diana's Bath'. The central arch frames a view of the succession of fountains that extends along the main perspective of the garden.

left, below and right *The spectacular vista laid out by Antonio Barbarigo in the seventeenth century. The fountains and statues were dedicated to the rivers and the winds and symbolize the order of an ideal universe.*

The garden consists of two long, straight, intersecting avenues, providing a sense of spaciousness which is accentuated by the fact that the level ground is undisturbed by terracing, embankments or steps. Nature is seen here not as some mysterious and impetuous force to be controlled but as a slow-moving regular system of seasonal change and development, just as time flows not like a tumultuous torrent but with the calmness and inevitability of a broad river: 'As its cradle the hill and its grave the sea', as an inscription reads beneath one of the two fountains dedicated to river gods. The garden may consequently be seen as a metaphorical celebration of the rhythms and order of nature.

This concept is exemplified by the stream which rises in a rocky spring at the top of one of the avenues and empties its waters into a basin at the foot of the stately pavilion known as Diana's Bath. The name of this imposing edifice is derived from the statue of Diana that surmounts it and towers over the whole garden. By association the garden of Barbarigo becomes the domain of Diana, that is of the realm of nature which mythology has always placed under her protection. The strict regularity and order of the garden plan are not to be taken, therefore, as a glorification of the power of man and art over the natural world but as a celebration of an ideal of nature from which disorder and the element of chance have been eliminated. On the top steps of the staircase leading to the villa are the words, 'You who arrive curious and wander from side to side seeking to satisfy a longing for rare charms, observe that any that can be found here owe everything to nature and nothing to Art.'

One of the 'rare charms' is certainly a unique rabbitry, an oval island complete with rococo pavilion occupied by dozens of ornamental rabbits and surmounted by an aviary for turtle doves, a place designed above all to surprise and delight. Its character extends to the whole garden: 'Here weeping has no place, laughter has its home'; 'The Graces rule where Pleasure reigns'. This devotion to pleasure is manifested in Barbarigo's riot of *giochi d'acqua*, water games and tricks devised to entertain, and in the intricacies of a magnificent boxwood labyrinth, a symbol of human error and deviation from the path of reason, but also and above all an invitation to indulgence and licentiousness. These features were forerunners of the spirit of hedonism which was to typify eighteenth-century Italian gardens.

The property passed from the Barbarigo family to the Michiel, Martinengo and Donà dalle Rose dynasties in turn, and lastly to the present owners, the Pizzoni Ardemani family, preserving intact that sense of peace and serenity which the Venetian patrician class sought from villa life, and which is contained in one last inscription: 'To achieve Leisure and Calm is the ultimate purpose of action.'

VILLA REALE

Marlia, Tuscany
Conti Pecci Blunt

'Well, Prince, so Genoa and Lucca are now just family estates of the Buonapartes.' This is the beginning of *War and Peace* and, as Harold Acton writes in his *Tuscan Villas*, it was also the beginning of the nineteenth-century vicissitudes of Villa Reale and its gardens.

In 1806 the small nearby town of Lucca became in fact the property not so much of the Buonaparte family as of Elisa Baciocchi, the ambitious, temperamental and philandering sister of Napoleon.

Lucca had until then offered little to social life but the benefits to be derived from its hot springs; it was an obligatory stopping place on those 'health tours' that carried illustrious convalescents across Italy from spa to spa. As Stendhal noted in 1829, 'This summer we shall spend fifteen days at the baths of Lucca . . .' But all that peace and leisure, however gilded, could hardly satisfy the demands of the new princess, soon nicknamed the 'Semiramide of Lucca' for the lavish prodigality of her court. One of her first concerns was to find herself a summer residence, and the choice fell on Villa Orsetti at Marlia. Count Orsetti was asked, indeed obliged, to sell the property that had been in his family since 1651, receiving in exchange

above A view of the villa from the great lawn laid out in the early nineteenth century.

right Pelargoniums on the terrace.

approximately half a million francs in silver, with which he indulged in a famously provocative gesture: he had the money melted down and cast into an immense silver service which he arranged to be carried on a cart beneath the princess's windows; he had word sent that if she looked out, she 'could see the villa of Marlia go by'!

Agostino Cerati described the Lucca villa in 1783 as divided 'into elegant gardens, artificially intermingled with little groves, shady paths and clear fountains where sylvan Nymphs and fountain Naiads never tire of roaming'. In fact, the upper part of the Marlia garden, the original nucleus which was laid out in the second half of the seventeenth century, consists of a series of interconnecting 'rooms' designed according to a late Renaissance architectural plan of great ingenuity: an intricate arrangement of alleys lined by high boxwood hedges ensures that each one is a surprise and a discovery.

From the façade of the villa itself stretches a huge lawn enclosed at the far end by a semicircle of tall boxwood. A garden room containing a magnificent fountain and grotto leads to an area planted with lemon trees, where a long basin of water reflects the lines of a balustrade culminating in a nymphaeum. A pathway leads from here to a little garden theatre planted in 1652, the finest example of its kind in Italy. It has a semicircular auditorium and a receding stage, complete with backcloth, wings and a prompter's box, permanently set with terracotta statues of Columbine, Harlequin and Pulcinella. Here 'the reigning Elisa sometimes fell into a swoon at my playing', as her chamber virtuoso Niccolò Paganini claimed.

Marlia, exquisite as it now was, could still not satisfy Elisa, who decided to endow her new possession with a vast romantic park of woods and groves inhabited by deer, the sort of Arcadian paradise she probably dreamt her whole principality might be. A lake was laid out in which the house and surrounding trees were reflected, creating a wide and magnificent vista from the villa itself. For this transformation Elisa relied indirectly on the advice of Louis Berthault, the architect who had designed the park of the Malmaison near Paris. Metternich, who visited the park in 1817, was enthusiastic: 'Marlia is a really divine place which Madame Elisa has had built and planted. The garden is wonderfully designed in the English fashion and is probably the only one of its kind, because I know of no other garden on this side of the Alps with such an abundance of trees and exotic flowers.' Indeed the princess had shipped her botanist off to the royal gardens of Naples to look for new species: weeping willows, mimosas, ginkgos, tulip trees and thuja were brought in to create those contrasts of colour and form which Berthault deemed 'necessary for the creation of a landscape garden, which must suggest in its design the imitation of nature'.

Further plans for enlarging the park, which would have involved the destruction of the seventeenth-century garden, were nipped in the bud only by the arrival in 1814 of English troops, putting an end to Elisa's reign and her dangerous romantic dreams. The villa was then acquired in turn by the Bourbons of Parma and the Princes of Capua. In 1923 it was bought by Count and Countess Pecci Blunt. Under their ownership the interior of the villa has recovered its neoclassical splendour, while the romantic park and the baroque garden have been sensitively and skilfully maintained.

92

preceding page *Pale blue plumbago spills over terracotta pots at either end of Villa Reale's arcaded loggia.*

above *The garden theatre, which dates from 1652.*

right and below *Fountains, pools, statuary and ornamental stonework form the nucleus of the original seventeenth-century garden. Round the walls of the nymphaeum are varieties of fuchsia, with bougainvillea and lemon trees in the foreground.*

LA GAMBERAIA

Settignano, Tuscany
Marcello Marchi

'In Florence, whenever you wanted to give an example of an enchanting, unforgettable garden, you mentioned the Gamberaia. Now the lovely garden has for the most part disappeared, the villa reduced to a heap of ruins.' These are the comments of Ginori Lisci in 1953. Eight years later, in *Italian Gardens*, Georgina Masson was able to write about the Gamberaia, 'today the garden is at once the loveliest and the most typically Tuscan I have seen.' What had taken place in the interim was in fact a small miracle, an extraordinarily meticulous and intelligent restoration of a historic garden almost completely destroyed in the war.

At the turn of the fifteenth century the villa was a simple country house owned by the nuns of San Martino, which subsequently became the home of the Gambarelli family and the Renaissance artists Antonio and Bernardo Rossellino. In 1618 it was bought by a rich merchant, Zanobi Lapi, who enlarged it in such a way that the simplicity of the original building was retained; the new villa, restrained and linear in style, is typically Florentine in its poise and composure. In 1717 the Gamberaia passed to the wealthy Capponi family who made only a few alterations to the house but were responsible for creating the garden proper.

Immediately behind the villa a long grass avenue, lined in its early stages by tall dark cypress trees, runs parallel to the façade; it extends from a shady grotto, where a massive statue of Neptune is concealed, to a terrace which opens out in bright sunlight on to a view of olive groves and vineyards. The avenue is flanked on one side by the villa and on the other by a high containing wall decorated with large figures that provide a rhythmic accompaniment to the gradual shift from the shade of the woods and the grotto to the light of the terrace and the open country.

On a level with the rear façade an opening in a wall leads to a small enclosed garden carved out of the hill at right angles to the house. Consisting entirely of an arrangement of pebbled paths and ornamental seashells adorned with statues and a rustic fountain, it is

preceding page *The parterre of La Gamberaia. The four long pools, originally lawns, were the innovation of Princess Ghyka, the sister of Natalia of Serbia, while today's owners have cut a series of arches in the semicircular boxwood hedge that frame distant views of Florence and the valley of the Arno.*

above *Geometric shapes against a wall of box screening one side of the garden.*

right *The pool and arcaded hedges enclosing the formal parterre make an effective contrast to the mass of roses clothing the outer walls of the garden (overleaf).*

an elegant variation on the nymphaeum theme. The design of this garden, and the shadows cast by its walls, create an air of seclusion and secrecy.

The south side of the villa looks on to the Gamberaia's famous Italian garden, originally an orchard. Towards the end of the last century the villa became the property of Princess Giovanna Ghyka, 'a narcissistic Rumanian lady', Bernard Berenson writes in his diary, 'who lived mysteriously, in love with herself perhaps and certainly with her growing creation, the garden of the Gamberaia'. It was thanks to the princess, advised by her inseparable companion Miss Blood, that the orchard became the masterpiece it is today. The geometric patterns of the flowerbeds, the rhythms established by the pots of lemon trees beside them, and the relationship between the different shapes of boxwood were accentuated and made infinitely more effective by the transformation of four large lawns into long mirror-like pools. Boxwood and hornbeam of different shapes were added to the existing hedges and blend together in a wonderful play of volumes reflected in the water. At the end is a semicircular pool protected by a high arcaded hedge, with views of the Florentine hills neatly framed by the archways.

The distribution of space, the balance of light and shade, the integration of the architecture with the contours of the surrounding landscape, all create a garden in which fifteenth-century geometric precepts, Renaissance principles of perspective and the baroque taste for drama merge into a harmonious whole: 'probably the most perfect example of a large effect obtained on a small scale', as Edith Wharton wrote in 1908.

During the Second World War the villa became a military map depot and was burnt down at the time of the German retreat. Nothing remained but the outside walls and an almost unrecognizable garden. The last owner, Mrs von Kettler, donated the desolate ruins to the Vatican which sold the property to Marcello Marchi in 1954. Restoration work continued for six years and was carried out with conscientious regard for the original plan. The profusion of roses growing among the boxwood hedges is a recent addition, creating a colourful contrast to the severity of the formal layout, and providing an eloquent testament to the devotion and love that went into the rebirth of the garden.

GEOMETRY AND GRACE

Giardino Giusti

Verona, Veneto
Conti Giusti del Giardino

The Giustis were a rich Tuscan family which the factional struggles between Guelphs and Ghibellines at the beginning of the fourteenth century had forced into exile in prosperous, secure and Ghibelline Verona. Within a hundred years, thanks to the success of their mills, they had become one of the wealthiest families in the city. Nobleman of the Grand Duke of Tuscany and Cavalier of the Venetian Republic, Agostino Giusti was cultured as well as powerful, an art patron and collector and a passionately devoted member of the Accademia Filarmonica. It was he who created this great garden sometime before 1570.

At the beginning of the eighteenth century, to celebrate its beauty and magnificence, the Giusti di Santa Maria branch of the family received the name Giusti del Giardino, meaning 'Giusti of the Garden', which they have retained ever since.

The basic plan of the garden consists of a broad, almost level area which rises gradually towards San Zeno in Monte and ends on the steep slope of the hill of San Pietro. A strict perspective discipline is established by a long and magnificent avenue of cypress trees dividing the parterre into two parts, each one of which is divided in

preceding pages *The great parterre of fountains, clipped hedges and elegant statuary was laid out in the sixteenth century according to strict Renaissance principles of perspective and symmetry, with long, straight avenues of cypresses and intersecting paths between the boxwood.*

above *The intricate pattern of hedges that makes up each section of the parterre was originally enclosed by tall cypresses, but the green rooms they contained were opened up in the eighteenth century when Lorenzo Muttoni's statues were installed.*

opposite *A snarling mask carved out of the tufa rock on the hillside, reminiscent of the figures of Bomarzo, lures the visitor into a mysterious grotto, a symbol of the darker side of the world of the Renaissance, which overlooks the formal, sunlit garden below.*

turn into square sections by intersecting cross paths. Each of these sections was originally enclosed by tall cypresses, creating a series of green rooms decorated with an arrangement of boxwood hedges, fountains and statues.

The visitor was invited to discover these rooms one after the other, strolling among Agostino's collection of Roman inscriptions, one of the most important of its kind in the Veneto region. Like those in the Cesarini garden-museum in Rome or the Corsini palace in Florence, they reconcile the ideas of classical antiquity, as reflected in the regularity of Giusti's broad vistas, with the charms of a garden 'Sacred to the Genius of Mirth, to the Muses and to Flora', as one of the inscriptions reads.

But this image of reason is shot through by wild, unruly rustlings of the late Renaissance in the form of an enormous stone mask whose shadow looms menacingly over the symmetry and clarity of the Italian garden from a site halfway up the rocky hillside. Below the mask is an artificial grotto carved out of the tufa. In this den, which seems to penetrate the deepest mysteries of the earth, the image of the visitor was disturbingly distorted by an ingenious play of mirrors. The grotto was connected to a long underground vault where the echoes of voices ricocheted from wall to wall, recalling the oracular lair of the pagan gods. This was the nocturnal world of the Renaissance, where a firm belief in reason was undermined by the mysteries and horrors of hostile nature, and security was entrusted to blind fate. In the Giardino Giusti, destiny is represented by the labyrinth which opens to the right of the garden, a representation of the human condition in which man is lost, both physically and metaphorically, in a world without prospects.

The present plan of the labyrinth, in which President de Brosses remained helplessly trapped for an hour, 'howling, unable to find my way, until the people of the house came to pull me out' (*Letter from Italy*, 25 July 1739), is the result of work carried out by the architect Luigi Trezza in the eighteenth century. The parterre was then opened out by the removal of the intersecting rows of cypresses, and the garden acquired elegant curvilinear beds in the French style, adorned with statues by Lorenzo Muttoni.

Giardino Giusti did not entirely escape the romantic craze of the nineteenth century, but the landscaping changes that took place then were soon reversed by the classicizing taste of the 1930s, which restored the original character of the lower, formal part of the garden. The random alterations that took place in the eighteenth century are now being corrected by Count Justo and Count Nicolo Giusti on the basis of historical research. With the help of the architect Pier Fausto Bagatti Valsecchi, they are gradually recovering the dual aspects of this remarkable Renaissance garden.

ROERO CASTLE

Guarene, Piedmont
Conte Umberto Provana di Collegno

In its architecture, its garden and its original owner, Roero Castle, between Monferrato and Langhe, is the very image of Piedmont in that eventful and despotic period, the eighteenth century. It was an age that began with the dukedom of Savoy becoming the kingdom of Sardinia, that saw the establishment of an absolutist state which always looked to France without being unduly influenced by it, and in which endless military campaigns were gradually replaced by brilliant theatre seasons. Victor Amadeus II enlisted the genius of Filippo Juvarra in the building of churches and palaces, Charles Emmanuel II had the new Teatro Regio built in Turin and the aristocracy laid down arms and hurried to court.

A brilliant dilettante, who handled his personal wealth and gifts with considerable skill, Count Carlo Giacinto Roero di Guarene was a worthy representative of his time. In 1707, at the age of thirty-two, he abandoned a military career to follow his natural inclinations for

drawing and architecture. He formed a close friendship with Juvarra and was greatly influenced by him. He also became one of the directors of the Teatro Regio and helped to make Turin one of the theatre capitals of Italy, along with Milan, Venice, Parma and Naples. He was the perfect eighteenth-century figure, multi-faceted and very Piedmontese in his balance between imagination and restraint, which was reflected in everything he did – including his most important achievement, the rebuilding of Roero Castle.

In 1725 Count Carlo Giacinto tore down the medieval castle at the centre of the family estate and began to rebuild it according to plans of his own. It was finished in 1780 and the property remained with the Roero di Guarenes until their line died out in 1899; it was then inherited by cousins, the Provana di Collegno family, and came down unaltered to Count Umberto, its present owner, who has preserved the property intact.

preceding pages *The main façade of the palazzo was designed by Count Carlo Giacinto Roero and completed in 1780. The garden is contemporary with the villa, and no changes have taken place to alter its original design: laid out on an axis with the building, its long straight paths converge towards the far end of the parterre, a dramatic device which accentuates the sense of perspective.*

right *Hedges of hornbeam and box and spires of clipped yew enliven the severity of the palazzo's façade. From the terrace the land falls away dramatically to the valley of the Tanaro river, leaving the outlines of the building and its garden sharply etched against the sky.*

Towering high on an isolated hilltop overlooking the Langhe countryside, it displays all the defensive strength of a feudal castle, but it also has a certain eighteenth-century elegance. The façade of the palace has long been attributed to Juvarra and his influence is clear, especially in the south front which looks on to the garden; it was designed in such a way as to create an ingenious interplay of projections and recesses that exploits to the full the warmth and colour of the Piedmontese brick facing. The lines of the south front are reflected in the plan of the garden, which consists only of boxwood hedges and clipped hornbeams and yew trees. The garden is relatively small and combines strict geometrical formality with a great feeling for the theatrical use of perspectives.

The central part is occupied by low hedges set around circular green lawns and areas of white gravel. The only other touch of colour in the garden derives from the warm red bricks of the palace. An imaginative, even rococo addition to this basic plan, which is so traditionally Italian in concept, is the series of tall yews clipped into layered pinnacles that soar high into the air. Their dynamic lines are echoed by high, clipped hornbeam hedges which surround the rectangular parterre and extend into a narrow neck following the central perspective line. This line is accentuated at its apex by the tall slender spires of two cypresses, below which the land falls away steeply, creating a feeling of infinite space beyond.

The influence of the school of Le Nôtre can be seen in the planting of yews at regular intervals in order to create 'cadences' that heighten the feeling of space, and in the perspective effects of the hornbeam hedges. But, as a contemporary art historian Marziano Bernardi has suggested, the original design of the garden, by Count Roero himself, may well have been further inspired by the theatrical genius of Bernardino Galliari, the prince of set designers at the Teatro Regio, whose visit to Roero in July 1755 is well documented: certainly the elegant balance and orderliness of the garden was enlivened by an inventive eighteenth-century theatrical imagination.

VILLA BELGIOIOSO

Merate, Lombardy
Marchese Annibale Brivio Sforza

above *A view from the staircase ornamented with reclining figures which links the piano nobile with the garden.*

preceding pages *The balustrade screening the lower part of the garden.*

Twenty miles distant from the city of Milan, in the foothills of Mount Brianza, can be seen the noble hamlet of Merate, in whose most lofty and beautiful position, overlooking the unending plain, stands the palace of His Excellency, the Signor Marchese Novati, Gentleman of the Bedchamber and General of the Line to Her Majesty the Queen of Hungary and Bohemia, who adding new delights to the merits of nature and the work of his predecessors, has made it deserving of universal wonder ... with its different gardens charmingly embellished with labyrinths, citrus fruits, fish ponds, fountains, statues, stairways, aviaries, porticos, prospects and pictures.

This was the way Marc'Antonio Dal Re described Villa Belgioioso in 1726 in his book of exquisite engravings of the palaces of Lombardy, *Villas of Delight*. His illustrations give a clear impression of the magnificence and elegant grandeur which must have contributed to the 'delight' of villa life in Lombardy in the first half of the eighteenth century.

In his engravings of the garden of Belgioioso, ladies and courtiers can be seen running between the jets of hidden fountains and strolling along avenues. The garden then consisted of six terraces, connected by staircases and balustrades, which provided intersecting vistas, each one culminating in a nymphaeum, a fountain or a niche adorned with a statue. The architectural complexity of the

classical Italian garden, of which this was one of the very last examples, can still be seen in these engravings, though Belgioioso's exaggerated geometrical formality and decorative touches already suggested the imminent appearance of ostentatious French-style flourishes and virtuosity. This first version of the garden was created by the architect Giacomo Muttone, who planned it for Marchese Ferrante Villani-Novati at the beginning of the eighteenth century. Of his design all that remains today is the first terrace, which runs along one side of the villa and is topped by a remarkable rococo balustrade carved in stone in the shape of logs.

In 1749 the villa was bought by Countess Barbara d'Adda, the wife of Prince Antonio Barbiano di Belgioioso. She was a cultured woman and a patron of the arts, who opened the doors of her Milanese palace to an 'Arcadian Colony' of poets and musicians, reviving the *précieux* spirit of the Parisian salons of the century before. Its courtly members, who adopted such names as Galatea and Nerina, Titiro and Melibeo, composed madrigals and minuets in the Countess's Lombardy gardens at Merate, Pavia, and Grumello.

In the latter half of the eighteenth century the villa acquired its present appearance and the garden was completely re-designed by an unknown architect. Flowerbeds were laid out in front of the house, with a broad expanse of lawn beyond them which slopes down from

above A circular pool reflects the clear architectural formality of the villa.
*below A great wide lawn lined with arcaded hornbeam hedges enhances the perspective effect of the
view from the villa.*

the façade and narrows as it does so, ending in an almost circular area of grass surrounded by gravel. The perspective effect of this long, wide lawn is accentuated by imposing hornbeam hedges clipped into continuous arcades (a direct reference to the Bernini colonnade in St Peter's Square in Rome) which run down either side and almost enclose the circular space beyond. A gap in the hedge on the far side of the circle, in a direct line with the villa, is occupied by an arc of statues, and beyond them the eye is carried on to a distant view of the Brianzoli hills. The clearly defined perspective and the solemnity of the composition can be attributed to the influence of the Le Nôtre school, but in the architectural quality of the lawns and hornbeam hedges the great Italian baroque garden can still be seen in all its magnificence, consisting more of contrasts of volume and space than of purely geometric patterns.

Almost all trace of the old Villani-Novati garden was finally obliterated in 1837 in favour of English-style landscaping, which still characterizes the area in front of the upper terrace. Grottoes, staircases and labyrinths were replaced by great clumps of trees and lawns, in compliance with the principle stated by the writer Francesco Milizia as early as 1797: 'A good garden is nothing but a little corner of nature embellished by art to reinforce the natural effect.'

Through the female line the villa passed in 1864 to the Trivulzio princes and, in this century, to Princess Marianna Trivulzio. She was married to Annibale Brivio Sforza who still lives there, maintaining the perfect balance between the elegance of the Italian garden, the grace of the late eighteenth-century adaptation and the peaceful shade of the surrounding park.

VILLA MOMBELLO

Imbersago, Lombardy
Principessa Sveva Pio Falcò

A nineteenth-century print of Mombello, which is kept in the villa, shows the building as it must originally have been, with a central block flanked by two wings, and a view commanding the whole Brianzolo countryside between Merate and Imbersago. The house was protected to the north by a long, dense row of hornbeams which probably enclosed an eighteenth-century geometric garden. Mombello in fact dates back to the first half of the eighteenth century, and was built by a Count Andreotti, who began work by enlarging an existing hunting lodge and ended up with one of the most sumptuous villas in Brianza. The story goes that the Count was then carried away by a ruinous passion for a Milanese ballerina and was forced to sell much of his property, including Mombello. So it was that the villa passed into the hands of the patrician Lombard Orsini

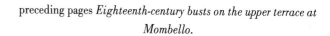

preceding pages *Eighteenth-century busts on the upper terrace at Mombello.*

above left *Ancient plane trees overlook the hedges and statuary of the terraces laid out by Prince Alfonso Pio Falcò.*

below left *The entrance gate to the courtyard at the back of the villa, which leads to the garden terraces.*

opposite *The loggia in front of the library opens on to the* giardino segreto, *or 'secret garden'.*

di Roma family. It remained with them until 1861, the year of the death of the last Orsini, Donna Beatrice, who had married Prince Antonio Valcarcèl Pio and named as her heir the latter's nephew, Don Giovanni Pio Falcò. In this way the villa became part of the estate of the Pio princes, grandees of Spain, who added magnificence and grandeur to its Lombard elegance.

While the villa was enriched over the years with works of art from both the Orsini Palace in Milan and the palace of the Pio princes in Madrid, the eighteenth-century garden was gradually transformed into a vast landscaped park planted with splendid plane trees. This park still exists today, extending over the northern slope of the hill above the villa. A formal garden probably lay to the south, in front of the house, but by 1920, when the last descendant of the Pio Falcò family, Prince Alfonso, began to take an interest in Mombello, all that remained of this part were three large terraces linked by stone staircases, the last remaining evidence of the elegance of the original plan. The rest was entirely given over to a vegetable garden.

So Prince Alfonso re-designed the whole garden, giving the three terraces a sense of the spaciousness and scale of the villa. The upper terrace is now an orderly parterre, where box hedges trace elegant arabesques on the gravel like notes drawn on a stave. The hedges on the second terrace are geometric in style, while on the third terrace the boxwood patterns have been replaced by clumps of marigolds, whose colours, along with the reds and pinks of a few *Lagerstroemia* trees, provide the only high notes in the composition. The terraces are enclosed by a long hornbeam hedge cut into archways which frame a view of the Brianza hills. This green wall is used not as a perspective device, as are the hedges at Villa Belgioioso, but rather as a means of screening the formal symmetry of the garden from the natural disarray of the park. Just beyond the hornbeam hedge, in the shelter of pines and cypresses, is a spacious rose garden to which the present Princess Sveva Pio Falcò devotes all her gardening attention.

Another small garden was laid out in front of the library which opens on to the first terrace by means of a long portico, whose archways are framed alternately by wistaria and mock jasmine (*Trachelospermum jasminoides*).

But the enchanting theatricality of the garden is apparent not so much from the terraces as from inside the villa: the curvilinear script of the box hedges echoes the curves of the decorative stuccowork inside; the stone stairways between the terraces meet between the windows of the galleries; the statues recall the same allegories and historical events as the paintings and frescoes on the walls of the rooms. And while light floods into these rooms from the garden, the Spanish elegance of the villa seems to enhance and complement the statues and stairways outside.

right Geometric patterns in boxwood echo the architectural formality of the villa.

VILLA AGNELLI

Villar Perosa, Piedmont
Giovanni & Marella Agnelli

above *The eighteenth-century façade of Villa Agnelli.*
opposite *Baskets of trailing ivy and terracotta pots overflowing with fuchsia line the walls of the elegant loggia.*
preceding pages *Filippo Juvarra's dome on the nearby church of Villar Perosa soars over the terrace in the upper part of the garden.*

A spirit inhabits the low-vaulted loggias, the galleries and terraces of Villa Agnelli, the spirit of Victor Amadeus II, Duke of Savoy and King of Sardinia. But the notion that this villa, set on a ridge separating two valleys in the Alpine foothills, had been built for the king is not supported by proof of any kind, only by clues. His image appears in the villa three times, in a bust, on a medallion and in a portrait. And another spirit keeps him company, that of Filippo Juvarra, whose grand staircase at Villa Madama in Turin is undoubtedly the model for the stairway connecting the two floors of the villa.

Only at the end of the eighteenth century is speculation replaced by reliable historical accounts, when Villar Perosa became in turn the property of Count Piccone, Governor of Asti, and of the Gamba and Turinetti families. In 1811 an Agnelli, a cavalry officer stationed at nearby Pinerolo, rented the villa and eventually bought it in 1853. It was here that Giovanni Agnelli, the founder of Fiat, was born thirteen years later: the elegant house, with its amazing stuccowork and delicate chinoiserie decorations, has been the home of all his heirs.

The original garden consisted of two terraces on the hill above the villa, a level open space at ground floor level and three long terraces below the house. The land then falls away very steeply into a wooded valley through which a stream runs. Until the end of the nineteenth century the lower terraces had been subjected to a series of transformations: as a result they were planted with trees of all kinds which cast shadows over a motley collection of flowerbeds, and stone basins were adorned with little fountains in keeping with a typically domestic nineteenth-century style. In 1955 Russell Page was asked to reorganize the whole garden: 'My first suggestion', the architect recalls, 'was to open up the garden to the light and atmosphere of the surrounding landscape.' So all excesses were removed and the terraces were laid out with regular beds full of roses. Nothing was allowed to obstruct the view of the Juvarra dome on the church of Villar Perosa or the contours of the mountains surrounding it. A statue of Diana the Huntress on the lowest terrace symbolizes the spirit of eighteenth-century grace which Russell Page's changes have recovered.

On the steep escarpment separating the terraces from the stream in the valley, Russell Page, at the suggestion of Donna Marella, has created an enormous and very beautiful wild garden, planted with rhododendrons, Exbury azaleas and magnolias. The shadier corners have been filled with bergenia, periwinkle (*Vinca minor*) and endless expanses of bluebells and lilies of the valley, which have together transformed the hillside.

Shade-loving plants gradually give way to water and bog plants as the garden descends to the stream that runs its entire length. Once a rushing torrent, the stream had to be restrained and a serene rhythm imposed upon it, so it was channelled into a series of pools of increasing size: the water falls in cascades from one level to the next, a pool contains it, it falls again and flows on, accompanied as it goes by a mixed planting of *Iris sibirica*, *Hemerocallis*, *Lythrum*, *Rosa hugonis*, *R. moyesii* and *Spiraea cantoniensis*.

The hillside, the valley, the stream and its pools represent a microcosm of the natural world, whose stillness echoes with birdsong and the sounds of croaking frogs under the shadows of Chilean pine trees, *Araucaria araucana*.

preceding pages *Clean, clear-cut architectural lines characterize the garden laid out to the rear of the house.*

left *Geometric simplicity gives way to a profusion of roses on the terraces planted by Russell Page.*

left and opposite *Diana the Huntress overlooks the formal beds of the lowest terrace, with* Prunus subhirtella *in full bloom beyond.*

left *Azaleas, acers and ferns in the wild garden that falls away steeply from the terraces to the valley below.*

overleaf *The banks of the stream have been skilfully planted with a range of water-loving species, including masses of* Iris sibirica.

LA PIETRA

Florence, Tuscany
Sir Harold Acton

'At present, Anglomania rules my plantomania', Catherine the Great wrote to Voltaire, and the quotation nicely expresses the explosive force of the landscaping craze, a real European passion which everywhere swept away the order and balance of the classical garden. Tuscany and Florence did not escape this revolution: the gardens of the Medici villas were spared, but in many others terraces and marble staircases gave way to hillocks, wooded groves and little temples. This was also the fate of La Pietra until an English family arrived at the turn of the century, destroyed all traces of English-style landscaping and re-established the character of the old Italian garden.

In 1460 the villa had become the property of Francesco Sassetti, banker to Lorenzo the Magnificent, who gave it the Renaissance features that are still to be seen in some of its very beautiful interiors. On his death La Pietra (The Stone), which takes its name from its position by the first milestone on the road from Florence to Bologna, was bought by the Capponi family. In the first half of the seventeenth century Cardinal Luigi Capponi had it enlarged, very likely entrusting the work to Carlo Fontana, who was responsible for the elegance of the sober baroque façade. The villa remained in the Capponi family for three hundred years, and when Florence became the temporary capital of Italy it was taken over by the Prussian Embassy. It was then that the Italian garden, laid out in a series of broad terraces, planted by the Sassettis and enlarged by the Capponis, was converted into an undistinguished wood in accordance with the contemporary vogue for landscaping.

In the very early years of this century Arthur and Hortense Acton bought La Pietra, which became one of the centres of that brilliant and cultured English colony which since the eighteenth century has made Tuscany its second home. 'If I could afford it', wrote Horace

opposite and below The baroque garden front of La Pietra, the work of Carlo Fontana, who carried out restoration work for Cardinal Luigi Capponi.

Mann in 1750, 'I really would take a villa near Florence, but I am afraid of its becoming a refuge for all the English.' And over the years many English and Americans were to migrate to Florence or 'Chiantishire', as the area came to be known, long before Ruskin published his *Florentine Mornings*. In Sir Arthur's day Bernard Berenson was living at I Tatti, Lady Cuffe Cutting at Villa Medici, Vernon Lee at Villa Palmerino, Sir Osbert Sitwell at Montegufoni … Many villas and their gardens owe their salvation to these new owners, whose wealth, sensitivity and culture, often scholarly, at times whimsical, brought about important restorations which revived a lost Renaissance classicism or baroque flamboyance.

So, starting in 1904, the garden of La Pietra was 'Tuscanized', as Sir Harold Acton recalls in his lively book *Tuscan Villas*. On the basis of drawings discovered in the Cabinet of Prints and Drawings in the Uffizi it was possible to reconstruct part of the original layout of terraces that once descended the slope behind the villa. Balustrades and staircases connecting three terraces were replaced and, as before, adorned with myrtle hedges and fountains. The loosely articulated plan combines baroque flourishes with a

left and opposite *A theatrical use of light and shade, space and volume, can be seen in the planting scheme of hedges of trimmed boxwood and in the placing of architectural features and garden statuary: these figures are the work of the Venetian sculptors Marinali and Bonazza.*

sophisticated use of light and shade, as can be seen in the contrast between the cool freshness of a grassy path shaded by a huge *Rosa banksiae* and the sunniness of a Corinthian colonnade set at the end of the garden. Great curtains of holm oak and cypress divide the open spaces, creating theatres which Sir Arthur ornamented with statues by Orazio Marinali and Tommaso Bonazza taken from the villas along the Brenta river, lending an exquisite Venetian liveliness to the grandeur of the garden. The orchard, which has remained unaltered, is enclosed by walls intricately decorated with coloured stones and pebbles; it opens out on to a large lemonery which blends the natural vitality of a true orchard with the elegant restraint of a sixteenth-century *giardino segreto*, or secret garden.

Honorary citizen of Florence, Sir Harold Acton still lives at La Pietra, and from its terraces he enjoys views which extend to the beautiful hills of Fiesole and San Domenico. The author of *The Last Medicis* and *The Bourbons of Naples* as well as *Tuscan Villas*, he is a man of great culture and erudition, qualities that have guided the restoration of both the garden and the villa, which under the terms of his will has been left to New York University.

Villa Balbianello

Lake Como, Lombardy
Conte Guido Monzino

'One can't describe the beauty of the Italian lakes, nor would one try if one could', Henry James wrote of Lake Como in his *Italian Hours*. And at the centre of the lake, considered its most beautiful part, on the Lavedo point between the bays of Diana and Venus, rises the Villa Balbianello.

The so-called 'mid-lake' area includes the promontory of Bellagio and, on the west bank, the coast which runs from the island of Comacina to Menaggio, beyond the Tremezzina shoreline. It is a place of sheer enchantment, with views of all three branches of the lake, and it became the summer haunt of cardinals and princes, from Paolo Giovio who built the first villa here in 1540 to Gian Angelo Medici who became Pope under the name of Pius IV.

The Giovio villa, Balbiano, was acquired in 1787 by Cardinal Angelo Maria Durini, papal legate and nuncio to Malta, Warsaw and Avignon. In order to enlarge the property he bought the promontory of Lavedo, a small peninsula jutting into the lake; its position and mild, sunny climate make this magical place, with its vineyards and olive groves, seem almost Mediterranean. On the Lavedo point stood a small church dedicated to St John and a little monastery of Franciscan friars, but it was not so much the spiritual allure of the spot as the captivating scenery which attracted the cardinal.

At the top of the small hill overlooking the water he built a portico of exquisite eighteenth-century elegance, open to the sun and breezes and flanked by two rooms, a library and a music room.

The delights of Balbianello and its spectacular views made it a

left *Punta di Lavedo and Villa Balbianello on the eastern shore of Lake Como. The ancient church and monastery, linked to Cardinal Durini's portico in the early nineteenth century, were transformed into a villa whose gardens now cover the promontory.*

overleaf *Steps and terraces follow the slope of the hill to the lake, and eighteenth-century statues overhung with plane trees, holm oaks and Scots pines, look out over the shimmering blue water.*

magnet for members of the élite, who at the end of the eighteenth century took holidays on the lake and enjoyed witty conversation, theatrical entertainments and recitals of Arcadian poetry and music.

In the following century Balbianello passed into the hands of the Porro Lambertenghi and Arconati Visconti families, becoming a hotbed of anti-Austrian conspiracy. At the entrance to the villa there was an *Arbutus menziesii*, the only plant in which green leaves, white flowers and red berries, the Italian national colours, appear at the same time. The patriot and dramatist Silvio Pellico (1788–1854) had just fled Balbianello when he was arrested in Milan. 'Blessed Balbianino!' he had written to his brother, 'I would spend my whole life there, so romantic, poetic and magical is this visit.'

Major works began in the early nineteenth century to restore the remains of the ancient monastery and church and to connect them to the portico, thereby transforming the group of buildings into a villa on various levels. It follows the slope of the hillside down to a little harbour tucked into an inlet. The house and its gardens suffered various turns of fate – and nearly finished in ruins – until in 1975 the property was bought by Count Guido Monzino, an explorer famous for his polar expeditions, and a man of culture. Under his care the villa was perfectly restored and the gardens brought back to what must have been their original splendour, of which nothing remained but the avenue of plane trees, the pines, an immense holm oak and the *Ficus pumila* covering the portico. Balbianello's magnificent situation allows a rare mixture of marine and alpine vegetation to flourish – some of the only specimens of Scots pine and *Trachycarpus spectabilis* in all of Lombardy for example. Its microclimate has made it possible to create a garden which, unlike many others on the lake, does not seek shelter by retreating inland but stretches out over the water.

The west bank of the promontory is covered by a carpet of laurel, which is regularly pruned so that it remains level with the lawn around the portico and creates an uninterrupted line flowing down to the water's edge. To ensure an unobstructed view of the house and the garden from the lake, and to frame the vista that extends to the far horizon, the promontory is planted with large, carefully tended specimens of hydrangea and azalea mixed with camphor and rosemary, leaving the space around the portico free. From the villa the eye follows an avenue of plane trees, crosses the sea of laurel, lingers on the roses which lean over the water by the landing-stage and is carried across the lake to the skyline.

THE ROMANTIC SPIRIT

Villa Melzi d'Eril

Bellagio, Lombardy
Conte Lodovico Gallarati Scotti

'Nothing in the world can compare to the charm of these days spent on the Milanese lakes', wrote Stendhal in 1817, referring to a trip on Lake Como that had carried him from shore to shore, all the way to Villa Melzi, south of Bellagio, where he was staying as a guest. The villa had been built in 1808–10 for Count Francesco Melzi d'Eril, upon whom Napoleon bestowed the title of Duke of Lodi. Melzi had lead the government of the short-lived Napoleonic Italian Republic (1802–5), becoming Lord Chancellor when the republic became a kingdom; in Stendhal's words, 'Under his rule the Kingdom of Italy was happier than France had ever been. It marched straight towards freedom.' From Napoleonic France Count Melzi received his neoclassical taste, which inspired both the choice of architect for his

above *A delicate domed pavilion with Moorish decoration, a perfect belvedere from which to enjoy spectacular views of Lake Como.*

right *A bank of azaleas and rhododendrons falls away to the shore, where pollarded planes stand out starkly against the milky waters of the lake.*

summer residence, Giocondo Albertolli, and the plan of the original nucleus of the garden, which Canonica and Villoresi helped to design.

White columns in pure Empire style flank the landing-stage in front of the villa, lending the view of the house from the lake an air of solemnity and classical monumentality. Along the shore to the left of the quay runs a long avenue of plane trees. 'Stirred always by gentle breezes, they filled me with pleasure and wonder', wrote the poet Davide Bertolotti in 1821. The axis along which the garden is laid out extends up the slope from the water to a high point above the villa, and is crossed by winding paths. Already by Bertolotti's time, as he describes, the garden was considered a marvel of 'rare foreign plants, fragrant shrubs and flowers of all kinds'. He was referring to those same specimens which, thanks to the care and devotion of Count Melzi's descendant, Count Lodovico Gallarati Scotti, are still a major feature of the garden. But the nineteenth-century imagination, with its romantic yearnings for strange and exotic places, identified the plants brought back from far distant countries with a vision of freedom, expansion and fabulous wealth: Japanese cedars (*Cryptomeria japonica*), Japanese maples (*Acer palmatum*), camphor trees (*Cinnamomum camphora*) and camellias were planted round the picturesque 'Japanese pool'; Emperor Maximilian of Hapsburg repaid the hospitality he had received at Villa Melzi with a few specimens of *Pinus montezumae*, whose branches reach out over the waters of the lake; from America came sequoias (*Sequoiadendron giganteum* and *Sequoia sempervirens*), tulip trees (*Liriodendron tulipifera*), red oaks (*Quercus borealis maxima*), Weymouth pines (*Pinus strobus*) and swamp cypresses (*Taxodium distichum*), and from the Caucausus came the Siberian elm (*Zelkova carpinifolia*).

Under the trees, at the intersections of the avenue and along the shore, are Egyptian sculptures, sphinxes and sarcophagi, Roman busts and statues by Giovan Battista Comolli, including a monument to Dante which inspired Liszt to write his Dante Sonata. But these marbles are not merely decorative; they give the garden an air of fantasy, turning it into a place of memories, dreams, desires and recollections, whether inspired by Dante, the Egyptian Pharaohs or the exotic and distant East.

Villa Melzi and its gardens bear witness to the refined taste of its owners and to the influence of an ineradicable cultural tradition which has held the wilder excesses of landscaping in check, restraining romantic disorder and bringing it into the confines of an ideal world of grace and unruffled tranquillity. 'The climate of villa civilization', wrote Mario Praz of Villa Melzi, 'lingers on, filling the rooms with a sweet and drowsy intimacy, spreading an aura of serenity about the gardens.'

Villa Camastra

Palermo, Sicily
Conte Lucio Tasca d'Almerita

In late December 1798 the frigate *Vanguard*, captained by Admiral Nelson, arrived in Palermo from Naples, which was then under threat of attack by French troops. The ship was carrying to safety Ferdinand I and his family, together with Lady Hamilton, and its arrival marked for the aristocratic society of Palermo the beginning of a brilliant season. Bourbon frivolity and flamboyance was to blend with the fashions and refinements brought by the English: such wealthy merchant families as the Whitakers, who established the Marsala wine trade, left an especially deep mark on nineteenth-century Palermo society. English influence was particularly noticeable in the gardens created in and around Palermo at that time, and a vogue for the English style spread with remarkable speed. At Bagheria, Piano dei Colli and Mezzomonreale the gardens of magnificent villas built by the seventeenth-century Sicilian aristocracy were re-designed entirely in the English style. The creation of the so-called Giardino Inglese in Palermo, a public garden designed by Basile in 1852, was followed by the gardens of Villa Camastra, the property of Count Tasca, and by Villa Sperlinga and Villa Malfitano, formerly owned by the Whitakers. They were not merely provincial imitations of a cosmopolitan vogue; they were examples of what became a very individual Sicilian and Mediterranean adaptation of the romantic garden. The subtropical climate allowed vegetation to flourish in a profusion and variety unimaginable elsewhere in Italy. The difficulty of keeping in check the disorder of this explosion of plant life was such that any desire to evoke contrasting emotions had inevitably to give way to a glorification of the energy of nature itself. The pursuit of romantic harmony therefore became a search for sublime rhapsody, and the results were sometimes overwhelming.

'The weather is magnificent and the garden entrances us again', Cosima Wagner wrote about a visit she made to Villa Camastra with her husband in 1881. Wagner himself wrote to Ludwig of Bavaria from Palermo, describing the 'stupendous country homes near the cities with incomparably beautiful gardens', and going on to boast of a 'particularly fond and devoted friend in Conte Almerita Tasca'.

Heir to a great fortune, enlightened innovator in the development of Sicilian agriculture, Lucio Tasca combined the spirit of the technocrat with that of the idealist. In 1839 he married Beatrice Lanza Branciforte, the daughter of Prince Butera and Trabia, a

preceding page *The entrance to Villa Camastra, where palm trees are underplanted with roses and iris. In the background are the rocky slopes that encircle the Bay of Palermo.*

below *A nineteenth-century gazebo in Moorish style, which frames a view of the semi-tropical garden.*

right *Water spills from a dolphin fountain into a pool planted with bamboo and papyrus.*

member of one of the most aristocratic and distinguished families in Sicily. She brought as her dowry Villa Camastra.

The house stands on the road from Palermo to Monreale, at the very heart of the Conca d'Oro, or 'Golden Shell' as the bay of Palermo is known. It was finished in 1777 for Donna Beatrice's father, with a garden laid out in geometric parterres. In 1855 Count Tasca transformed the parterres, filling the area with every conceivable variety of rare semitropical plant. The result was not so much a romantic garden as an exotic botanical collection: towering *Araucaria bidwilli* and *Cunninghamia* blended with *Livistona chinensis*, rubber plants (*Ficus elastica*) and *Corippa australis*; beneath the palms grew dwarf senecios, encircled by orange *Echeveria derenbergii* and *Scirpus cernuus*, surrounded by cinerarias and *Russellia juncea*, some of which still survive. A

below *A classical urn among the dark green leaves of* Chamaedorea, *with arum lilies in the foreground.*

right *A magnificent specimen of* Ficus macrophylla, *whose rope-like aerial roots have thickened into massive serpentine ground roots that extend for several metres, helping to support the wide-spreading branches and incidentally providing a sheltered nest for a swan.*

distinctly romantic flavour was provided by little temples, statues and pillars celebrating classical mythology or the mysteries of nature. To the right of the villa a pond was laid out in the shade of a gigantic *Ficus macrophylla*, whose aerial roots reflected in the water seem to impart to the whole garden an atmosphere of luxuriance and exoticism which is almost alarmingly potent.

Even in the thirteenth century there were countless gardens around Palermo – 'like gems around a woman's throat', as a contemporary Arab chronicler described them. The garden of Villa Camastra, thanks to the care and attention of the Tasca d'Almerita family, has remained intact, one of the very few not to have been laid waste in a city where the only thing that does not seem to change is the magnificent Sicilian sky.

NINFA

Sermoneta, Lazio
Roffredo Caetani Foundation

'A medieval Pompeii' was the way Ferdinand Gregorovius described the ruins of the town of Ninfa in his historic *Passeggiate d'Italia* (Italian strolls). But while Pompeii was buried by lava in a single day and life cut off forever in a matter of seconds, Ninfa (the word means nymph in Italian) suffered a slow decline, besieged in turn by medieval troops and waves of malaria, and finally brought down by the passage of time. Its towers and churches were abandoned to the heavy air of the Pontine marshes, and gradually nature took it over, enfolding it in ivy and brambles.

In the distant past it was considered to be a place of magic, its lake inhabited by nymphs and benevolent gods. Pliny in his *Historia naturalis* tells of islands which revolved on the lake to the strains of magical music. But this pastoral idyll was swept away in the Middle Ages. Domain of the counts of Tusculum, it passed in the twelfth century to the noble Frangipani family who built seven churches and a second wall to enclose the city, which had expanded beyond its original limits. On 20 September 1159 Alexander II, threatened by the antipope Honorius IV, was brought here and crowned Pope in the main church, Santa Maria. As retribution for this, the city was besieged and sacked by the troops of Frederick Barbarossa. A century later the Annibaldi family, which had succeeded the Frangipanis as rulers of Ninfa, sullied its own good name with a famous act of treason by handing over Conradin, Duke of Swabia, to Charles of Anjou, who had him beheaded in Naples soon after, in 1268. Legend has it that Ninfa, the daughter of Giovanni Frangipani, fell in love with the prisoner Conradin, and at the news of his death threw herself off the tower into the lake. Since then the beautiful Ninfa has appeared on the water every evening to mourn her love, and the river that flows through the town is said to be the tears that she sheds for him. So the nymphs of classical times were replaced by sorrowing ghosts, tokens of the altered fortunes of the city. In 1297 Ninfa was bought by the Caetani family of Pope Boniface VIII, and became the scene of violent family struggles. In 1382 it was sacked again and never recovered.

Remarkably, the villa has always remained the property of the Caetani family. In 1922, at the time of the major scheme for the reclamation of the Pontine marshes, Prince Gelasio Caetani, determined to save Ninfa from total decay, set about draining the marshes on his property, not in order to recover its former beauty but to protect the romantic appeal of its ruins. Prince Gelasio died in

preceding page *Ninfa, the 'city of dreams', was finally deserted in the fourteenth century after repeated sackings and malarial epidemics. It remained abandoned until 1922, when Prince Gelasio Caetani, whose family had owned the property since 1297, began to drain the marshland on which it stands. Its ruins still survive, clothed in a mass of ivy, and creamy sprays of* Cotoneaster *now spill through gaps in the medieval walls and arum lilies flower along the banks of the river.*

left *Steep, parched hills form a protective backdrop to this well-watered valley, where wild flowers sprinkle the grass under the delicate pink sprays of* Cornus florida rubra.

opposite *The ruins of Ninfa's old city hall have been restored, and the building is now the headquarters of the Caetani Foundation, though of the original walls and seven churches only fragments remain, covered in climbing hydrangea (*Hydrangea petiolaris*), clematis and old roses.*

right *According to legend, the waters of the river that flows through the valley are the tears shed by Ninfa Frangipani for her lover Conradin. Behind the bridge, which is known as the Ponte del Macello, runs the castellated city wall, its merlons now shrouded in greenery.*

below *The sculptural leaves of* Gunnera manicata, *indigenous to the Amazon jungle, spill over the river, which is spanned at this point by a fragile wooden bridge.*

opposite *A well-established specimen of* Rosa *'Kiftsgate' climbs the cypresses planted by Prince Gelasio Caetani.*

1935 and his work was taken up with great imagination and skill by his brother's wife, Donna Margherita Caetani, who helped to turn the 'city of dreams', as Ninfa was traditionally known, into one of the most beautiful gardens of Europe, its gentle slopes covering almost twenty acres.

Everyone who knew Margherita Caetani speaks of her radiant personality and great culture and her exceptional gift of intuition. Descendant of a New England family, she was described by virtue of her beauty and disposition as a Henry James figure: her passion for everything new and adventurous was held in check by the firm conservatism of her Bostonian background, and the garden she created is the perfect expression of this equilibrium. Among the ruins, around the towers and along the crenellated walls, multitudes of old roses, iris and magnolia were planted, chosen with the same sensitivity that is to be found in the choice of authors she published in her literary magazines, *Commerce* and *Botteghe oscure*.

Ninfa is sheltered by high hills, and the stream that runs through it ensures its fertility: the trees planted by Prince Gelasio, maples and cypresses in particular, already look centuries old, while roses climb up the ruins and cascade into the clear waters of the stream, *Rosa banksiae* smothering the remains of Santa Maria and white *R.* 'Kiftsgate' winding about the cypresses. Carpets of columbines and peonies paint an impressionistic backdrop to ancient towers covered with moss and clematis.

This is the result of a project completed by Margherita's painter daughter, Donna Lelia, and her husband, Hubert Howard, a member of the family of the Dukes of Norfolk; until his recent death he lived at Ninfa and ran the Caetani Foundation, of which the garden is a part. While Donna Margherita was a brilliant and gifted nature lover, Donna Lelia was a scholarly gardener with a real botanical talent, and the extraordinary variety of plants in this garden is largely her doing, the fruit of years of passionate devotion, from 1945 to 1976.

What has been destroyed by time here has not been restored, but what has remained has been preserved. The ruins of the ancient town are no longer simply historical relics but an essential part of the spirit and atmosphere of Ninfa, which is perhaps the quintessential romantic garden.

Villa Rufolo

Ravello, Campania

The second act of Wagner's *Parsifal* is set in the gardens of Klingsor, on an enchanted summer night heavy with the scent of flowers; the inspiration for the setting came to Wagner one May day in 1880 when he stepped into the garden of Villa Rufolo. Since then the images of northern mythology have overlapped those of the Mediterranean on this sunlit southern coast, introducing rich Amalfi merchants and Anjou princes to the Knights of the Holy Grail. This is only the most recent association of a garden in which literary and stylistic influences of all kinds have met and interacted, suspending it halfway between legend and reality.

Villa Rufolo stands high on the rocky Amalfi coastline, which Boccaccio (1313–75) describes in the Second Day of the *Decameron*: 'A coast which overlooks the sea, and which the inhabitants there call the Coast of Amalfi, is studded with little towns, gardens and fountains, and inhabited by men of wealth.' And he goes on to say: 'Among these towns there is one called Ravello which, like today, was inhabited by wealthy men; the richest of all was Landolfo Rufolo by name.'

The Rufolos were undoubtedly one of the most illustrious and distinguished of the rich Amalfi families. They produced four bishops, and their fortune, founded at the time of the Republic, reached its peak with Matteo Rufolo, banker to Charles of Anjou, whose crown he even held in pawn. It was a wealth created by trade based on Amalfi's strategic importance as a maritime centre in the twelfth and thirteenth centuries. Its position, at the crossroads between East and West, the confluence of the Arab world and Christendom, brought it invaluable commercial and cultural riches. Like Norman Sicily, Ravello produced its own delightful combination of Moorish and Romanesque art and architecture, of which Villa Rufolo is one of the most famous examples.

Guarded by two towers and protected by a high wall, the villa

right A view over the palms and pine trees of Villa Rufolo to the Gulf of Salerno. Today the villa belongs to the State.

overleaf The spacious sun-filled terrace looks out to the mountains around Ravello, an area whose princely life was described by Boccaccio in the fourteenth century.

stands alongside Ravello Cathedral. From the outside it has all the severity of a medieval fortress, but once one has entered the garden through the tower gate, this first impression instantly gives way to a sense of quiet contemplation, springing largely from the character and situation of the garden itself. It is laid out on different levels round a secular cloister, and retains much of the atmosphere of a medieval garden.

In the design and decoration of the arcaded upper gallery along one side of the cloister the Moorish spirit of the villa can be seen in all its intricate delicacy and charm: slender twin marble columns support a sinuous interlacing of arabesque ornament whose grace and rhythm seems to animate the whole garden. The capitals have plant forms which are complemented by the leaves of the many palm trees; stone roses peer out from the arcading and real roses climb the pergolas facing the sea; the curves above the arches are picked up by pathways leading through ferns and hibiscus to secluded pavilions. The atmosphere of the garden is carried through into the villa itself,

left *Steps lead down from the upper to the lower terrace, where a network of paths divides beds planted with palms, roses, bergenias and yuccas.*

right *The cloister, whose elegant curvilinear decoration combines elements of Arab and Norman architecture in a style unique to southern Italy.*

to the ancient Gothic dining hall, the oratory and the Hall of the Knights, whose basilica plan reveals the villa's Roman origins.

In the mid-eighteenth century Villa Rufolo underwent extensive and drastic alterations which included, among other things, destruction of part of the cloister to make room for the kitchens. However in 1851 the property was bought by Francis Neville Reid, a Scotsman who called in Michele Ruggiero (he was later put in charge of excavations at Pompeii) to carry out restoration work and recover the original balance of Roman, Moorish and Romanesque influences in the villa and its garden. The new owner and his architect were as careful and meticulous in doing so as Lord Grimthorpe would be extravagant and eccentric half a century later in creating the nearby Villa Cimbrone, and today Villa Rufolo is a testament not only to the craftsmanship and cultures that produced it but also to the sensitivity and care that have preserved it intact.

VILLA FOGAZZARO

Oria, Lombardy
Marchese Giuseppe Roi

above *Lake Lugano and the foothills of the Alps*
from the waterside terrace of Villa Fogazzaro.

opposite *Cypresses surround the villa and a* Ficus pumila
tumbles over the wall that runs along the water's edge.

'Close to the steep mountain vineyards strewn with olive trees, the villa straddles the path skirting the lake and plunges straight into the water. Its simple façade looks west towards the village of Oria, with a little hanging garden on two levels . . .' This is the description by Antonio Fogazzaro of the home of Franco, Luisa and little Ombretta, the leading characters in his novel *Piccolo mondo antico*; it is set here, in his mother's dearly loved house in Valsolda on the eastern branch of Lake Lugano, near the Swiss border. The path, the little garden, the villa, everything in this brief quotation illustrates the sense of nineteenth-century domesticity and intimacy which suffuses the house and garden; both the fabric of the place and its atmosphere have been devoutly preserved by children and grandchildren, as they are today by Giuseppe Roi, the writer's great-grandson.

The lake lies between the steep slopes of the Alpine foothills, and yet enjoys a microclimate in which olives, pines and cypresses thrive, as they do in the garden itself, along with two strange and lonely palm trees that no one dares to touch: they might have been planted by the writer and that is enough to ensure their preservation. The garden extends along the shore on three terraces adorned with boxwood, climbing roses, *Osmanthus fragrans* and a white plumbago, and a *Ficus pumila* covers the balustrade between the garden and the lake, falling gracefully to the water. Colours and scents seem to fill the garden, as Fogazzaro described in a letter he wrote in the summer of 1864: 'The weather rolls on magnificently, so warm that our little garden has still not been touched by frost and is all flowers and vegetables, smelling sweetly of roses and vanilla.'

VILLA TRITONE

Sorrento, Campania
Mariano & Rita Pane

Villa Tritone stands high above the sea on the rocky cliffs of the Sorrento promontory, facing over the Bay of Naples to Capri. The views are veiled by a bright haze in the summer that allows one only to guess at the outlines of Vesuvius and Punta Scutolo across the bay. According to the legend recounted by Pliny and Strabo, the sirens Parthenope, Leucia and Lygea lived on this shore, and the beauty of the place has lured poets, painters and hedonists ever since; it was the summer haunt of Roman patricians and is still a place for romantic holidays and pleasure. Stendhal, without unnecessary elaboration, describes it simply as 'the most beautiful place on earth', and passes on to other matters.

Immediately beneath the villa, almost at water level, stairs and passages carved in the rock reveal the presence above of what was once an important Roman villa with nymphaeums and pools; it is thought to have belonged to Agrippa Postumus, the nephew of Augustus. In the sixteenth century a convent was built there for the nuns of St Clare, and was later taken over by the Jesuits who planted a grove of citrus trees around it. In 1888 the Labonia barons transformed the convent into a villa.

By then Sorrento had become the fashionable summer meeting place of the most brilliant cosmopolitan society. In its gardens Ibsen wrote *Ghosts* and Wagner worked on the composition of *Parsifal*. But the villa did not come fully into its own until the beginning of the century. William Waldorf Astor, scion of a family so wealthy that it was known as 'the landlords of New York', bought the property in 1903. He was a restless man: ambassador to Rome in 1882, he became an English citizen fifteen years later (and was made a viscount in 1916), and fell in love with Sorrento where he spent long periods of time. A contemporary of Henry James, he could have stepped right out of the pages of *The Ambassadors*, which was published in the year he bought the villa.

He gave the main façade of the house a classical character, which was animated by the vaguely neo-Gothic lines of the windows, revealing a certain eclecticism of taste. The garden, however, is

left *Neoclassical heads sculpted by Alma Tadema (1836–1912) adorn the balustrade of Villa Tritone's belvedere, with its wide open view of Capri and the Bay of Naples.*

overleaf *Arches cut into the wall that screens the garden from the bay allow enticing glimpses of the view that has drawn poets and painters here for centuries. Palms, cacti, yuccas and other succulents line the paths with a mass of semi-tropical vegetation, and wistaria winds its thick, woody stems over the stonework round the windows.*

distinctly Mediterranean in style: it was created by Lord Astor and provides the perfect setting for his magnificent collection of archaeological finds, which are surrounded and sometimes shrouded by a lush growth of palms, ferns, agaves and orange trees that scent the air and filter the sunlight.

An unusual architectural feature of the garden, and a brilliant scenic device, is the high stone wall that extends along the side facing the sea, closing off the view. Rather than display the whole vast panorama of the celebrated vista all at once, narrow arched openings buried in wistaria afford brief glimpses of the bay, which are all the more enticing for being incomplete. The stone arches framing each view seem to enhance the magic of the scenery by lending it a quality of distance and inaccessibility. In this way the garden is concen-

trated and contained within itself instead of opening out to the sea and thereby losing some of its potency, just as one's gaze, instead of wandering to the far horizon, is concentrated on the treasures of the garden: a lovely sixteenth-century fountain at the end of an avenue of *Chamaedorea* and *Tritonia crocata*, a statue of Neptune hidden in a stand of yuccas, or an Early Christian sarcophagus resting on two Corinthian capitals. An abundance of ferns, fuchsias and agapanthus grow beneath low walls covered with *Ficus pumila*.

In the mid-Twenties the villa passed into the hands of the Dutch Embassy, and from 1943 to 1945 Benedetto Croce lived here during the bombing of Naples. 'I can't manage to make myself comfortable in this place,' he wrote to a friend as soon as he arrived, 'which looks like neither my middle-class home nor your aristocratic but traditional one.' Subsequent owners have nonetheless managed to make themselves comfortable at Villa Tritone. It is now the property of Mariano and Rita Pane who have carried on the work of Lord Astor, enhancing the garden with a rare collection of palm trees, from *Dasylirion* to *Chamaerops humilis*, and skilfully uniting its Mediterranean and classical elements in a semi-tropical luxuriance.

preceding pages *A shady avenue of* Chamaedorea, *with the vivid orange flowers of* Tritonia crocata *below and* Rosa banksiae *on the pergola above, leads to a stone fountain dating from the sixteenth century.*

above *A narrow path meanders between* Dracaena, *ferns and agaves, and the fronds of palm trees meet overhead, providing a cool, deep shade from the dazzling southern sunlight.*

right *A fine specimen of* Agave attenuata.

below *An Early Christian sarcophagus carved with the figures of a husband and wife, one of the garden's many links with the distant past.*

overleaf *The reticulated stone wall and lion mask above the sarcophagus.*

MODERN INSPIRATIONS

VILLA PUCCI

Granaiolo, Tuscany
Marchese & Marchesa Emilio Pucci

Villa Pucci is a large country mansion of fourteenth-century origin, set on top of a hill and surrounded by a wide expanse of woodland. It has been the home of the Pucci family since it started life as a small fortification defending the land around Castelfiorentino, near Empoli. The exterior, as is often the case in Tuscany, is at once simple and imposing: its central section rises through three storeys to an open gallery above, and the plain off-white walls are pierced by windows framed in blue-grey sandstone. At the beginning of this century a traditional Italian garden was laid out in front of the villa, with the usual array of formal flowerbeds and fountains, and even a few palm trees. In 1970 the designer Emilio Pucci decided to restructure it completely, and turned to Gae Aulenti for advice. 'How could it be', the architect now recalls, 'that somebody not only believed in the drawings I presented, but actually decided to make the garden I designed?'

The plan called for the total destruction of the garden that then existed, in favour of one huge lawn cut to its full width into a series of broad shallow steps following the slope of the hill from the house to the surrounding woods. The garden became an architectural space complementing the linear simplicity of the villa and creating an image of extraordinary purity, austere and self-assured, and based on a strict geometric rationale. The Pucci garden could have been designed by Descartes for the ideal city described in his *Discourse on Method*, or it might have been included in Abbot Ferrari's seventeenth-century treatise on gardens to illustrate the 'square garden', which was meant to symbolize eternal stability.

The great wide steps across the lawn are edged in stone to accentuate the horizontal emphasis of the garden and the play of linear perspectives. The lines of stone are the simple graphic highlighting of the natural slope of the hill, denoting the lie of the land like contour lines on a map. Seen from the villa, they seem to be the emanations of a natural force spreading outwards and driving away the natural disorder of the woods, while from below they follow and lend rhythmic flow to the gradual rise of the hill towards the villa.

This very modern though essentially traditional garden, which came about through the meeting of a great architect and a great stylist, seems to make some intriguing connections, combining allusions to Land Art of the 1960s, in which areas of coastline or landscape were treated as art, with the lesson of Francesco di Giorgio Martini on the Italian Renaissance garden: 'The planner must strive to reduce nature to some kind of perfect figure, such as circular, square or triangular.'

below and opposite The majestic Tuscan home of the Pucci family, set in an architectural garden designed by Gae Aulenti.

SAN LIBERATO

Bracciano, Lazio
Contessa Maria Sanminiatelli

'Green fingers are a question of fact, and remain a mystery only to those who are not gardeners. They are an extension of the heart. A good garden cannot be created by someone who has not the capacity to know and to love growing things.' Landscape architect Russell Page wrote these words two years before meeting the owner of San Liberato, yet they could have been written with him in mind. Art historian and naturalist Donato Sanminiatelli had spent his early life in Chile, where he devoted himself to the study of plants, and trees in particular, which were his true passion. In 1961 he had the opportunity to express this passion fully when he and his wife, Maria Odescalchi, built a country house on a large estate overlooking Lake Bracciano. It stands in a huge natural amphitheatre surrounded by chestnut forests.

The house was planned in such a way that the Romanesque simplicity of the little church of San Liberato nearby, a place of worship since ancient times, would not be disturbed. It is now swathed in sweet-smelling mock jasmine (*Trachelospermum jasminoides*) and Clair Matin roses. The woods beyond the amphitheatre were closed off by the planting of a belt of specimen trees, which provide a contrast to the indigenous varieties and in so doing serve to contain the garden.

Russell Page began work at San Liberato in 1964, laying out the garden on the slopes that extend from the house to the lake and the woods. The first thing to be done was to introduce a series of features that would break the uniformity of the slope to the woods. Rather than levelling the whole area, the effect of the incline was enhanced by the creation of an almost level lawn in front of the house, from which the land could fall in two steep drops to terraces and then slope gently down to the shadows of the woods. This plan offered suitable areas for the planting of a variety of species, and allowed for a border to be laid out between the house and the lake. Filled with lavender, pomegranates, old roses and *Lagerstroemia*, this border provides a focal point, holding the eye before letting it follow the lure of the sparkling light on the water. To the right the downward sweep of the land is interrupted only by islands of shrubs, including spiraea, weigela and hypericum.

To connect the house to the woods an avenue was laid out with borders of Iceberg roses; it extends in a straight line to two large beds filled with magnolia underplanted with white bergenia and agapanthus, and then runs on to the damp shade of the chestnut grove. The pale transparent blue of the agapanthus is the only touch of colour in a mass of white blooms. Russell Page created this part of the garden as a tribute to Maria Sanminiatelli, who complemented her husband's botanical passion with a sensitive appreciation for subtle harmonies of colour. In 1980, when Countess Maria was left a widow, she – a gardener by vocation and a botanist by necessity – chose to transform the area of the garden near the church of San Liberato, previously given over to the experimental raising of annuals; she planted it instead with borders of *Senecio leucostachis*, *Taphiolepis indica*, *Teucrium fruticans* and *Cerastium tomentosum*, whose delicate greys and blues blend beautifully with the mellow grey stone walls of the church.

opposite and below *A soft haze of roses and valerian, part of the planting scheme introduced by Russell Page in the 1960s.*

A collection of specimen trees such as Liriodendron tulipifera (above)
and Liquidambar styraciflua and Gingko biloba (right) have been
planted to screen the garden from the chestnut woods that surround it.

FRESCOT

Turin, Piedmont
Giovanni & Marella Agnelli

Frescot, protected by the foothills of the Piedmontese Alps, stands on the edge of Turin, and from the low wall that encloses the garden the eye can range over the entire city. In a small area the property comprises a rose garden, an orchard and a vegetable garden, its plants contained by low box hedges that divide the space according to a straightforward geometric plan. The design is sophisticated to the point of simplicity, and contributes to an atmosphere of peace and relaxation, the perfect contrast to the life of the city below.

In 1766 the house was acquired by Francesco Ladatte, sculptor to the court of Victor Amadeus (he carved the famous stag that surmounts the royal hunting lodge, the Stupinigi Palace near Turin). Ladatte's studio at Frescot was soon enlarged to make room for the studios of his artist daughter, Rosalia, and his son-in-law, Vittorio Cignaroli, an arcadian landscape painter; with their son, Angelo Antonio Cignaroli, also an artist, they lived and worked there until 1800. The property was then sold to the Frescot family, and artistic zeal gave way to the bourgeois tranquillity of nineteenth-century domestic life, not so much inspiring as comfortable. Eventually, however, both the artistic energy and the domestic ease that had once pervaded Frescot evaporated, and the house became little more than a ruin in a wood. In the 1960s it was bought by the Agnellis, who made it their town house.

The garden, laid out between the two wings of the house and surrounded by espaliered apple and pear trees, is the creation of Donna Marella. It is divided into four parterres with boxwood borders, one side filled with *Rosa multiflora* 'Cin-Cin' and the other with an array of vegetables, hedged in by sweet-smelling lavender and backed by the snow-white rambler *Rosa* 'Albéric Barbier'. At the far end of the parterre a small door leads from the enclosed and elegant world of the garden into a spacious park of majestic chestnut trees.

right and overleaf Rosa multiflora *'Cin-Cin', planted beneath clipped pear trees in beds enclosed by box hedges and a border of lavender. The peaceful, domestic garden is protected by woodland and, to the north and west, by the Torinese hills.*

Palazzo Querini Stampalia

Venice, Veneto
Querini Stampalia Foundation

above Carlo Scarpa's formal architectural design for this walled garden in the heart of Venice, seen from the top of the palazzo.

opposite Water falls steadily from the outlet of a narrow canal into a marble basin, whose decoration of concentric circles repeats the shape of the round stone well above it.

overleaf The bright white flowers of a spiraea stand out against the dark ivy clothing the brick walls of Querini Stampalia. A pattern of ornamental stonework runs the length of the courtyard like a frieze, its measured regularity enhancing the sense of harmony and calm that pervades the garden, and which it owes largely to the influence of the Orient.

Every architectural creation in Venice is conceived in terms of water – the shifting, sometimes gentle, sometimes treacherous flow of water that eats away the mortar and the stone. The canals, bridges, alleyways and little squares form a closely-woven web of interconnecting spaces in which the light is constantly changing, making dazzling patterns on the water that reflect on the façades of the palaces, and fading to a cool, secretive shade in the well of a building or a narrow passageway. Venetian gardens are almost always set in a courtyard at the end of an alley or canal, where light can expand and be absorbed by plants and stone and water. They offer a welcome respite, especially in summer, from the confinement of Venice's network of narrow streets, like taking a deep breath after a run. The Venetians, who created three hundred and fifty gardens in the seventeenth century, were well aware of this, as was Carlo Scarpa who in the early 1960s planned the garden of the Querini Stampalia Foundation.

The famous Venetian architect, a close friend of Frank Lloyd Wright, was engaged to restructure the garden and ground floor of the building, one of the oldest Gothic palaces in Venice, after severe flood damage. He devised a system of channels on the ground floor so that water can meander inside the building as well as outside: this was a stroke of genius, depriving the water of its destructive force and turning it into a shining, light-giving, carefully-controlled link between the exterior and the interior.

The garden, to the rear of the building, is enclosed by high walls and lies parallel to the canal which runs along the façade. The theme of water and light predominate in the garden too, where a narrow channel flows into a small maze-like fountain, runs along a raised canal and falls gently into a basin of Istrian marble. In following this course it seems to describe a symbolic process of purification: from the fountain, which has a built-in filter system, it emerges cleansed and pure, and the marble basin where it comes to rest is made up of concentric circles, an image of harmony reminiscent of the gardens of the Orient.

Set in one corner is a great square fountain, also Oriental in inspiration, consisting of a mosaic pool holding a basin ornamented with copper. The water spills gently from the basin to the pool, dripping in a quiet, regular rhythm, all the surfaces reflecting and diffusing the glowing Venetian light. A long band of laminated tiles in grey, ochre and black, set into a cement panel, closes off one side of the garden and acts as an additional reflective surface, mirroring the transparent water in the small canal.

The central area of the garden is occupied by a lawn planted with a cherry tree, a magnolia and a pomegranate, which bloom in turn from March to June. Along the walls are spiraea, laurel, myrtle and periwinkle, and in one corner a specimen of the aromatic allspice shrub (*Calycanthus*). The secret of Scarpa's garden is suggested by a fragment of his own conversation: 'In Venice you pass through very narrow passageways, and then there's that wealth of water and open space ...'

LA FERRIERA

Capalbio, Tuscany
Conte & Contessa Antonello Pietromarchi

Italian gardens are usually enclosed, protected places that shrink from disorder and shut out the natural world around them with hedges and high walls. By contrast the garden at Capalbio is open to the flat lands of the Maremma that surround it, a coastal stretch of Tuscany which in the intense heat of summer is bathed in dazzling light and in the winter swept by frosts and bitter winds.

When in 1968 Antonello and Giuppi Pietromarchi decided to restore the large building which served as the manor house of a sixteenth-century iron foundry (*ferriera*), the garden was in a state of dereliction. In front of the house was a large pine wood and all around it nothing but olive trees. The character of the place derives largely from the spirit of the surrounding landscape, and nothing has been done to disturb it. The woods and olive groves have been left intact. The pine trees shelter the house from the worst of the winter gales, and help to cool the blistering heat of summer, while the olives, with their gnarled and twisted trunks, are an essential, timeless feature of the hills and plains of Tuscany. In their soft silver

glow has been planted a collection of old roses which have taken on the easy, accidental shapes of the olive trees, the delicate shades of *Rosa* 'Apricot Nectar' and *R.* 'Gloire des Mousseux' seeming to lend a touch of elegance to the surrounding countryside.

From the end of the olive grove a flight of steps, bordered by *Rosa* 'Albéric Barbier', climbs to a terrace along the side of the house. Here too there are olives but around each tree a circular bed has been filled with roses and fuchsia, *Echium fastuosum* and Chilean jasmine (*Mandevilla suaveolens*) which flower in succession. From here a path leads through a 'blue garden' filled with great pots of plumbago, *Hibiscus syriacus* 'Blue Bird' and agapanthus. Beyond, in a small secret garden, between *Erythrina crista-galli* and *Rosa banksiae*, is a large Jerusalem thorn (*Parkinsonia aculeata*) which in July is covered with a mass of small sweet-smelling yellow flowers.

From here a path leads back to the terrace along the house, where the dense planting of shrubs of many varieties makes a decorative display of shapes and textures, revealing not only a botanical passion but also a love for the routine tasks of gardening – the pruning, grafting, training and general care – that every year produces such wonderful sights as the dazzling profusion of enormous white blooms on the guelder rose (*Viburnum opulus*).

As the Viennese writer Hugo von Hofmannsthal wrote in 1906, 'there is nothing that reveals the spirit more than a garden where the mind of the gardener is always actively engaged'. There is no doubt that the spirit of Giuppi Pietromarchi is revealed in her garden and that her mind is engaged in the aesthetics of its design, in the welfare of her plants, and the maintenance of the delicate balance that exists between Capalbio and the surrounding landscape. Her passion for plants is one that she pursues wherever she goes: once in a little nursery near Nairobi she discovered a white rose she had never seen before and asked its name. It was known as 'Giuseppina Sgaravatti', which was her own maiden name. The rose, created at the turn of the century as a tribute to Giuppi's grandmother, had probably been taken to Africa by a missionary and had bloomed there, forgotten by the family until she rediscovered it and brought it back to Capalbio.

left Agapanthus under the silver-green leaves of olive trees.

right Typically Mediterranean plants such as oleander and umbrella pines thrive in La Ferriera's harsh Maremma climate.

VALLE PINCIOLE

Cetona, Tuscany
Federico Forquet

above *A distant view of Valle Pinciole on its Tuscan hilltop.*

right *A pergola covered with* Rosa bracteata *and bordered with* Iris
'Lady Isle' on the second terrace leads to a terracotta figure of 'Winter'
backed by cypresses.

above *The pergola recalls Tuscan gardens of the fifteenth century, such as Il Trebbio, which used red bricks known as* pianelle *in the building of similar cylindrical piers.*

below *The perfumed herb garden leads to a walled room in which* Rosa *'Constance Spry' grows among the branches of an ancient olive encircled by* Hosta fortunei.

opposite *Columnar cypresses and* Rosa × alba *frame the foreground of a view of the surrounding hills.*

The spirit of the Cetona landscape is encapsulated in the painting by Perugino, *The Adoration of the Magi*, which hangs in the Oratorio S. Maria dei Bianchi in Città della Pieve, the artist's native town. The delicacy of light and colour in his depiction of the Umbrian landscape, with its gentle hills and acacia trees and winding country tracks, is typical of the land between Cortona and Orvieto, where St Francis and St Benedict preached. Federico Forquet's house lies at the heart of this beautiful region.

The building is divided into two parts, originally a farmhouse and a toolshed, which in 1970 were connected by a wall, creating a small courtyard that leads to the living room and to another room beyond, not for family or guests but for geraniums. The garden is divided into a series of garden 'rooms' open to the sky, small spaces that reflect the infinite scale and variety of the surrounding landscape. In the country round Cetona the views of little hills and valleys change at every turn of the road, only rarely widening into broad panoramas, and the rooms of the garden similarly disclose their secrets one by one, so that new discoveries can be made through every archway and down every path. The first room is enclosed by four low walls and planted with a collection of sweet-smelling red geraniums, fuchsias, peonies and hostas. A small door on the far side leads to a perfumed garden, a room full of medicinal herbs such as tarragon, lavender, sage and rosemary, surrounded by drifts of woodruff (*Galium odoratum*) and white dead nettle (*Lamium album*). The last room is devoted entirely to white flowers – *Magnolia × highdownensis*, *Hydrangea petiolaris*, white agapanthus and *Carpenteria californica*.

Other garden rooms are separated not by walls but by different levels, which were originally terraced for growing vines. Federico Forquet and Matteo Spinola, who participated in the planning of the garden, kept the terraces intact as a reminder of the original character and purpose of the property, and as a structural framework for new planting. Initially the garden extended only to the first terrace, which was filled to the brim with around three hundred species of rose. They bloom magnificently in the chalk soil of this area and make a spectacular display. Over the years all the terraces have been incorporated into the garden, not according to any formal plan but in order to create a patchwork quilt of colour that has gradually unfolded down the hillside.

A maze on the second terrace leads to a room lined with lamb's tongue (*Stachys lanata*) that forms a silver carpet covered in June with countless mauve flowers. A narrow passageway then leads to a small area planted with neat pomegranate trees, and continues under the shade of a pergola, edged by Hidcote lavender and covered with climbing roses. Three more rooms, divided by boxwood hedges, have been laid out on the last level, where the sense of harmony and peace that pervades the whole garden seems to be concentrated: varieties of iris in every subtle shade of blue and purple are interspersed with lavender blue *Nepeta mussinii* and shaded by Red Sentinel crab apple trees.

right *Terracotta pots containing* Buxus microphylla compacta *between a vine-covered pergola and* Rosa *'Nevada'.*

opposite *The creamy yellow flowers of* Iris *'Olympic Torch' overlook the boxwood labyrinth on the terrace below.*

below right *Varieties of iris – 'Pacific Panorama', 'High Above' and 'Intriguer' – border a path under Red Sentinel crab apple trees.*

above *The delicate papery flowers of* Papaver orientale *'Perry's White'*.

opposite *From the lowest terrace the garden looks out to the open countryside.*

below *The silver-pink blooms of* Rosa Regensburg.

GARAVICCHIO
AND THE TAROT GARDEN

Capalbio, Tuscany
Principe Carlo Caracciolo di Castagneto
& Don Nicola Caracciolo di Castagneto

The entrance to the Garavicchio villa, framed by two silver wattles (*Acacia dealbata*) and flanked by an Arab jasmine (*Jasminum sambac*) and a pink trumpet vine (*Bignonia capreolata*), opens on to a small garden on three levels that descends to the scorched, brackish marshlands of the far southern fringes of the Tuscan Maremma. In the distance the coast arches away south from Monte Argentario to the shores of Etruria, Montalto and Tarquinia.

Half a mile or so from Capalbio is the border between Tuscany and Lazio, the ancient frontier between what were once the Grand Duchy and the Papal States. It is said that the name Garavicchio derives from Guardia Vecchia (or Old Guard) and that the place might once have been a guardhouse, possibly connected to the large customs house nearby. That it stands on a hill could well be explained by the fact that the whole of this coastal plain was infested until comparatively recently by malaria.

In 1943 the house was bought and converted by Marchese Litta, while the basic plan of the garden was designed by Marchesa Maria Luisa Bourbon del Monte. Prince Filippo Caracciolo di Castagneto took over the property in 1960, as a seaside and country residence. In its present form the Garavicchio garden is largely the work of Carlo Caracciolo, and it combines a typically Anglo-Saxon botanical emphasis with the exuberance of a Mediterranean garden. The terrace in front of the main façade of the villa was walled in to separate it from the surrounding olive grove and to create the private and protected atmosphere typical of a medieval *hortus conclusus* (or garden enclosed). It is planted with large specimens of sage (*Salvia leucantha*), *Verbena officinalis* and *Osmanthus fragrans*, and with agapanthus and plumbagos whose soft blues melt into drifts of pale mauve and white Japanese anemones (*Anemone hupehensis*) and fuchsias (*Fuchsia magellanica*), the aromatic scents of herbs and lemon trees blending with sweet-scented buddleia and jasmine. A path leads through a long pergola to the lowest terrace, which is divided into two parts by a lawn. The first part is intersected by a

preceding pages The great figure of the Angel representing Temperance in Niki de St Phalle's Tarot Garden.

above left The Garavicchio villa, surrounded by cypresses and umbrella pines, on its hill above the coastal plain

left Terracotta pots overflowing with Campanula isophylla *on the terrace of the Garavicchio garden.*

opposite The lowest terrace, where valerian blends with the old roses planted by Marchesa Bourbon del Monte in the 1940s.

above and below *Old roses drift into the olive groves that extend towards the sea beyond Capalbio, and tumble over the walls of the terraces round the house.*

below *The dark entrance to the figure of the Magician, and the sphinx-like Empress against a background of the flat scrubland of the Maremma.*

opposite *The figure of the Sun, inspired by the imagery of primitive art, surrealism and magic.*

border of valerian and miniature roses and protected by a rose-covered wall edged with tobacco plants (*Nicotiana*) and Angel's Trumpet (*Datura cornigera*). Marchesa Bourbon del Monte had already planted a collection of old roses here, together with many varieties of iris, and a border of blue and grey plants – lavender, *Buddleia*, *Senecio*, *Ballota pseudodictamnus* and *Teucrium* – has been added. Their soft, indefinable shades fade into the silver glow of the olive groves stretching out towards the open country and the sea beyond. A new corner of the garden, planted in pale blues and yellows with plumbago, *Ceratostigma*, lavender and *Helichrysum angustifolium*, has been laid out around the pool by Oliva di Collobiano.

Years ago Niki de Saint Phalle, a friend of the Caracciolo family, had a dream: she was strolling in an enchanted garden inhabited by benevolent, magical figures which seemed to loom up out of the ground, clothed in fantastic colours and decked with precious stones. In a natural amphitheatre in the scrubland around Garavicchio she was offered the opportunity to realize her dream and there she created the 'Tarot Garden'. Among the olives, cork oaks (*Quercus suber*) and mastic trees (*Pistacia lentiscus*), larger and larger statues have sprung up at her bidding: Tarot card figures – the Magician, Justice, the Sun, the Castle (which represents the Emperor) – their bases plunged deep into the earth, cast weird shadows and awesome magic spells over the surrounding scenery, catching the light of the sun in pieces of mirror glass and coloured ceramics that encrust them like a carapace. The animal and plant kingdoms seem to merge in these extraordinary figures so that trees become snakes, sphinxes are part mermaid, birds turn into angels, emulating the mystery of the Sacred Grove of Bomarzo and the colourful sensuality of Gaudi's Catalan gardens. They follow no logical order, and just as one card follows another apparently at random in a game of tarot, so each person takes a course through the garden that reflects, if not his fate, at least his imagination. The Tarot Garden is a place to let the mind wander at will, drawn on by the lure of the unexpected that encourages the visitor to drift and lose his way in a dream world.

above *The Castle, a symbol of power, its angular form contrasting with the sinuous lines of the other statues of the Tarot Garden. A sculpture by Jean Tinguely represents a thunderbolt striking the top of the tower.*

opposite *The Magician, or 'Homage to Bomarzo', clothed in Murano glass and a mosaic of vividly coloured ceramics and mirror glass. Behind can be seen the Tower and the scarlet Rocket.*

LA FOCE

Chianciano Terme, Tuscany
Marchesa Iris Origo

'In a desert they have created a palace with every up-to-date luxury and a garden of great beauty. Through a sheer effort of will, a land which seemed entirely barren has been made to flower.' This could sound like the report of an astonished traveller describing the work of some pioneer in a remote corner of the New World; instead it is Bernard Berenson commenting on the achievement of Antonio Origo and his wife, Iris, who in Val d'Orcia, a few miles from Chianciano Terme, made a garden in one of the most desolate areas of Tuscany.

Iris Origo was the daughter of cultured and wealthy New York parents. When her father, Bayard Cutting, a brilliant diplomat, died in 1911, her mother, Lady Sybil Cuffe, moved with her daughter to Florence, and took up residence at Villa Medici, once the favourite abode of Lorenzo the Magnificent. The villa and its gardens soon became one of the centres of that brilliant 'hypersophisticated and hyperintellectual' English and American society that in Florence revolved around Bernard Berenson and his numerous guests, Vernon Lee, Edith Wharton, Robert Trevelyan, Lytton Strachey and Bertrand Russell. 'The immediate effect of finding myself exposed so intensely to so much culture', Iris Origo recalls, 'was that I soon reached the point of associating all talk about Florentine coffers or garden plans with a feeling of boredom that was to stay with me up to the time I bought a house and garden of my own, when I discovered I possessed a knowledge that I had consciously suppressed.'

In 1924 Iris married Antonio Origo and in true pioneer spirit they decided to devote their energies to the transformation of virgin territory, where everything had to be created out of nothing. Iris recalls their adventure in *Images and Shadows*, a witty, courageous and charming book: 'We both wanted to escape city life and lead

right The sixteenth-century inn transformed into a villa in the 1920s by Iris and Antonio Origo.

right *A belt of cypresses softens the contrast between the strict regularity of the formal walled garden, with its boxwood hedges and lemon trees in terracotta pots, and the hills of the Val d'Orcia beyond.*

overleaf *A view from the top of the garden of the winding road up the hillside, planted with cypresses in imitation of the landscapes depicted in fourteenth-century Tuscan paintings.*

what struck us as a pastoral Virgilian existence.' It was then that they discovered a 3,500-acre estate, a 'lunar, bleached and inhuman' landscape intersected by low clay hills known as *crete*, worn by the wind and inhabited by a few tenant farmers and their families who offered prayers to St Fisco Fosco, an imaginary and terrible saint who hated the poor and had to be placated by these poverty-stricken people. 'To stop the erosion of those steep hills, to transform that bare clay into fields of grain – that, we were sure, was the life that we wanted.'

A large late sixteenth-century inn became the manor house, named La Foce (The Outlet) because it was situated at the confluence of two valleys, the Val d'Orcia and the Val di Chiana. In this wasteland the dream of having a garden must have represented for Iris Origo the most direct link to her infancy and childhood, which had been filled with wonderful gardens. Her paternal grandparents lived in Westbrook, on the south shore of Long Island, where they had assembled one of the finest collections of exotic plants in the United States, while the house of her maternal grandparents in Ireland was set in the midst of a large, mysterious and unruly romantic garden.

The opportunity for Iris to put her 'consciously suppressed' knowledge to use came when her paternal grandmother first visited La Foce, and was surprised by the great shortage of water. She supplied the necessary funds to build a pipeline to bring an abundant supply of water to the house, and it was then that creating a garden became a real possibility. To this end Iris enlisted the help of the architect Cecil Pinsent, who in Florence had restored the gardens of Berenson's villa, I Tatti, and those of Villa Medici and Le Balze. Pinsent abided by the golden rules of historic Italian gardens, exploiting the natural unevenness of the land to create a flexible succession of levels and formal terraces which acted purely as elements of transition between the architectural lines of the house and the broad views of the Val d'Orcia stretching away on all sides. The severity of the plan reflects that classical spirit which in the early decades of this century was often embraced by English scholars and architects, who defended the Italian tradition against attack from the persisting fashion for landscaping. A rose garden was set out one level higher, parallel to this series of terraces, and bordered by a long pergola covered with wistaria that extends along the hill to the shade of the woodlands. Here, where there was once nothing but clay, grow maidenhair ferns, pomegranates and peonies, lavender hedges and tufts of thyme, rose bushes and dense thickets of broom. A land which seemed entirely barren has indeed been made to flower.

BIBLIOGRAPHY

Acton, Harold: *Tuscan Villas*, Thames & Hudson, London 1973

Alberti, Leon Battista: *Dell'Architettura* (P. Portoghesi), Milan 1966

Argan, Giulio Carlo: *Voce* 'Giardino e Parco' in *Enc. Univ. dell'Arte* vol. X

Assunto, Rosario: *Il Paesaggio e l'Estetica*, Naples 1973

Azzi Visentini, Margherita: *L'Orto Botanico di Padova e il giardino del Rinascimento*, Milan 1984

Bagatti Valsecchi, Pier Fausto: 'Tipologia della Villa Italiana', *Ville d'Italia*, Milan 1972

Baltrusaitis, Jurgis: *Aberrations*, Paris 1957

Bascapé, Giacomo: *Arte e Storia dei Giardini di Lombardia*, Milan 1962

Battisti, Eugenio: *L'Antirinascimento*, Milan 1962

Belli Barsali, Isabella: *La villa a Lucca dal XV al XIX secolo*, Rome 1964

Belli Barsali, I. and Branchetti, M. G.: *Ville della campagna romana*, Milan 1975

Borsi, F. and Pampaloni, G.: *Ville e Giardini d'Italia*, Novara 1984

Bruschi, Arnaldo: *Il Problema storico di Bomarzo* 'Palladio' XII, 1–4, Milan 1963

Chastel, André: *Arte e Umanesimo a Firenze*, Turin 1964

Coffin, David: *The Villa in the Life of Renaissance Rome*, Princeton University Press, Rome 1979

   The Italian Garden, Dumbarton Oaks, Washington 1972

Cruciani, Boriosi: *La realizzazione barocca del Giardino Italiano*, Antichità Viva 2, 1963

Dal Re, Marc-Antonio: *Ville di delizia nello stato di Milano (1726–43)*, Milan 1963

Dami, Luigi: *Il giardino Italiano*, Milan 1924; Brentanos, New York 1925

Fagiolo, Marcello: *Natura e Artificio*, Rome 1979

   La città effimera e l'universo artificiale del giardino, Rome 1980

Fariello, Francesco: *Architettura dei giardini*, Rome 1967

Ferrari, Gian Battista: *Flora ovvero cultura dei fiori*, Rome 1638

Gothein, Marie Luise: *A history of Garden Art (1926)*, New York 1979

Gromort, Georges: *L'art des jardins*, Paris 1934

Latham, C.: *The Gardens of Italy*, Newnes, London 1925

Masson, Georgina: *Italian Gardens*, Thames & Hudson, London 1961

Ministry of Culture: *Giardini Italiani, note di storia e di conservazione*, Rome 1981

Nobile, Bianca Marta: *I giardini d'Italia*, Bologna 1984

Page, Russell: *The Education of a Gardener*, Collins, London and Glasgow 1962

Pindemonte, Ippolito: *Su i giardini inglesi*, 1818

Pizzetti, Ippolito and Cocker, H.: *Il libro dei fiori*, Milan 1968

Porcinai, P. and Mordini C.: *Giardini d'Occidente e d'Oriente*, Milan 1962

Praz, Mario: *Bellezza e Bizzarria*, Milan 1960

   Il giardino dei sensi, Milan 1975

Ragionieri, G.: *Il Giardino Storico Italiano*, Florence 1981

Recchi, M.: *La villa e il giardino nei concetto della Rinascita*, in Critica d'Arte 1937

Shepherd, J. C. and Jellicoe, G.: *Italian Gardens of the Renaissance*, E. Benn, London 1925

Silva, Ercole: *Dell'arte dei giardini inglesi (1813)*, G. Venturi, Milan 1976

Tafuri, Manfredi: *Il mito naturalistico nel Cinquecento*, L'Arte, 1, 1968

Tagliolini, Alessandro: *I giardini di Roma*, Rome 1980

Venturi, Gianni: *Le scene dell'Eden*, Ferrara 1979

Wharton, Edith: *Italian Villas and their Gardens*, Bodley Head, London 1904

ACKNOWLEDGMENTS

Marella Agnelli and her associate contributors would like to thank the following for their co-operation and kindness during the preparation of this book:

Dottore Gian Lupo Osti

Barone Architetto Pier Fausto Bagatti Valsecchi

Signora Henriette Chiesa

Baronessa Alessandra Casana

Marchesa Lavinia Gallarati Scotti

Dottore Giuseppe Orlando

Architetto Paolo Pejrone

Signora Marisa Sgaravatti

Architetto Paolo Sgaravatti

INDEX

Numbers in italics refer to illustrations

221

preceding pages *The Renaissance parterre at Giardino Giusti, one of the finest gardens of the Veneto.*